Women
ON
THE RISE

Pivotal points to success
shared by members of
RISE Collaborative Workspace

Stacy Taubman and Kate Wiegmann

Women on the RISE
Pivotal points to success shared by
members of RISE Collaborative Workspace
Stacy Taubman and Kate Wiegmann

Published by On the RISE Press, St. Louis, MO
Copyright ©2018 Stacy Taubman and Kate Wiegmann
All rights reserved.

Cover design: Stephanie Sabo
Cover photo: Kathleen Mortland
Project management and interior design: Davis Creative, DavisCreative.com

Library of Congress Cataloging-in-Publication Data
Library of Congress Control Number: 2018932377
Stacy Taubman and Kate Wiegmann
Women on the RISE: Pivotal points to success shared by members of
   RISE Collaborative Workspace
ISBN: 9780999752500
Library of Congress subject headings:
   1. BUS109000: Business & Economics/Women in Business 2. SEL027000:
      Self-Help/Personal Growth/Success 3. BUS025000: Business &
      Economics/Entrepreneurship

2018

This book is dedicated to the countless women and men
who helped make RISE Collaborative Workspace
a reality. Without their support and inspiration
our community, workspace, and this book would
never have been possible.

Our Greatest Fear

It is our light not our darkness that most frightens us

Our deepest fear is not that we are inadequate.

Our deepest fear is that we are powerful beyond measure.

It is our light not our darkness that most frightens us.

*We ask ourselves, who am I to be brilliant,
gorgeous, talented and fabulous?*

Actually, who are you not to be?

Your playing small does not serve the world.

*There's nothing enlightened about shrinking so that
other people won't feel insecure around you.*

It's not just in some of us; it's in everyone.

*And as we let our own light shine,
we unconsciously give other people
permission to do the same.*

*As we are liberated from our own fear,
Our presence automatically liberates others.*

—Marianne Williamson
Excerpt, "A Return to Love"

Foreword

By Mary Jo Gorman, M.D., M.B.A.

I am unapologetically passionate about seeing women succeed.

When a woman has a dream, the only greater satisfaction than watching her achieve it is to be a part of her journey. I was able to be a small part of Stacy Taubman's journey in opening RISE Collaborative and seeing the community she has built has been a joy.

I first met Stacy for coffee in December of 2015. At that time, she shared with me her vision for a place for women of all ages to come together to build community, connections, and confidence. She wanted to build a pipeline of success for women and teen girls who want more for themselves and those around them. Stacy imagined something, much more than a functional place to work and meet, but a place to support other women in achieving their own success.

I was so impressed with her vision and energy that I agreed to mentor her once a month to support in her entrepreneurial journey. From refining her financial model to navigating the process of securing outside investment, I supported Stacy as she worked through the details of building out her business.

Any successful career is a long and arduous path and there are many opportunities for mistakes. Women often choose small business, corporate paths and entrepreneurship to succeed. I've seen many capable professional women make a variety of mistakes: fail to develop their network, rely on the wrong "experts" or proceed without getting feedback and wisdom from others. People "don't know what they don't know," and that's why I have put my energy into educating women on their career paths, so they can advocate for themselves and make decisions that increase their chance for success.

It takes many and varied resources to build a community of successful, professional women. In addition to Brazen St. Louis, which focuses on growth seeking female entrepreneurs, and RISE Collaborative, it's great to have another resource for women who are striving to achieve their dreams. As an added resource, the stories in this book are important. They give you, the reader, a chance to learn from other hard-working women and hopefully, make one less mistake. Professional success depends upon making more right decisions than wrong ones—or at least making big right decisions and small wrong ones! By courageously sharing their unique journeys of missteps and lessons, failures and successes, they are making an important contribution to your success.

I am proud to have played a role in supporting Stacy along her journey to open RISE Collaborative. When women support each other, incredible things happen. I hope you are as moved by this collection of stories as I am and that you, too, pursue what you want and need in your life.

Mary Jo Gorman, M.D., M.B.A
Chairman of the Board, Brazen St. Louis

Contents

Introduction

At RISE Collaborative, we live by the quote, "You are the average of the five people you spend the most time with," by Jim Rohn. We all have had that friend or family member who leaves us feeling less than or defeated. Imagine the opposite: spending time with people who not only make you feel like the impossible is actually quite possible, but they want to help make it a reality. Those are the people we want to spend time with and can make a measurable difference in our lives.

In creating RISE Collaborative—a story you'll hear more about in the first chapter—we set out to create a pipeline for success for women of all ages. A place where women can come to build authentic community and connections. The women who join our community share a few things in common. They are ambitious and driven. They are curious and creative. They're also flawed and unafraid to be vulnerable. And they all want to see the other women around them succeed—because when you succeed, so do they.

We all come to this community with our own experiences, wounds, successes, failures, lessons learned and goals to be met. And unlike other spaces in our personal and professional worlds, we come to this community valuing collaboration over competition. We check our "sharp elbows" at the door and open ourselves up to knowledge, referrals, conversation, and supporting one another.

In the stories that follow, you'll hear from 17 women. Each have a story to tell about a journey that shaped them, and pivotal points that fundamentally changed the way they viewed themselves, their world, and led them to where they are today.

Wherever you are in your journey, we hope this book helps shape you too.

Stacy Taubman   Kate Wiegmann
Founder/CEO   Partner/COO

Connecting the Dots

One of my favorite paintings is *A Sunday Afternoon on the Island of La Grande Jatte* by George Seurat. This beautiful image was created using a technique of painting called "pointillism" where the artist uses only individual dots—millions of them—to create a masterpiece.

For the non-artists out there like myself, let's take a minute to wrap our heads around what that process would be like.

At the beginning, I can imagine the dots on the sprawling blank page must look sporadic and disconnected. A casual observer to this painstaking process would have no clue what it would end up looking like and be skeptical at best—doubtful at worst. I'm sure even the artist has moments of doubt that the points will all come together. And it wouldn't be until the painting was nearly complete that the general public would actually get it.

Welcome to the world of being an entrepreneur! Or really anyone who is pursuing a dream and it's exactly how I've felt over the last five years going from Educator to Entrepreneur and opening RISE Collaborative Workspace.

Five years ago I would have bristled if anyone used the word "entrepreneur" to describe me. Now, I would actually tell you I'm not only a serial entrepreneur, but have been one from a very young age. I just didn't know it.

To fully understand my journey of opening RISE Collaborative Workspace, you have to rewind to my college days and my first "dots" on the page.

I vividly remember my ADHD kicking in during an especially dull college math class and instead daydreaming about the dreaded question, "What do I want to be when I grow up?" The two responses that came to mind were "CEO of a company" or "Principal of a high school."

I find it comical that at that time, I didn't know "CEO" stood for "Chief Executive Officer." All I knew was that it meant "boss" and clearly that was important to me...!

Opting to pursue the occupation I could actually define, I decided to double major in Math and Math Education. I graduated, got my first job, and started my Masters in Administration almost immediately out of college. And although I was definitely putting "dots" on my canvas, they weren't quite coming together as I thought they would.

After finishing that Masters and interning in the Principal's office, I quickly realized I wasn't cut out to be a principal. I started painting more seemingly-random dots on the canvas and switched directions, getting my Masters in School Counseling. I wasn't ready to completely jump ship from Education and I thought being a School Counselor would mean I'd get to be the "good guy" and talk about life all day with my students, which sounded way better than being the "bad guy" principal and handing out detentions!

(Well, we all know how this one ends, considering this is the story of how I opened RISE Collaborative...!)

At this point, I was 33, had been teaching for 12 years, had two undergraduate degrees, and now two Masters, but not one clue as to what I wanted to be when I grew up. I was completely burned out from teaching and was floundering in so many areas of my life.

The one thing I did know was I felt the most alive when I was helping young people figure out who they were and what they wanted from life. I guess it is true that we teach what we most need to learn.

It's also true that life sends you pretty loud messages from time to time, and some of them are incredibly painful. My loud message occurred in the summer of 2012 when a young woman from the school I taught at committed suicide. Watching the aftermath of this tragedy and teaching/counseling her friends became a tipping point in my life. It made me realize it was time for a change.

High school really sucks for a lot of students, and especially girls. They are faced with so many mixed messages and pressures. It took this truly awful event to help me find my next step: to start a company that helped high school girls feel a sense of belonging, joy, and confidence. Something I'd struggled with at their age (and let's be honest...throughout adulthood, too) and something I knew I was uniquely qualified to do.

Let me rephrase that: I was uniquely qualified for the *impact* part. The *business ownership* part—that was a different story. I had no formal business training—unless you can count Business 123 in college, which basically taught me how to balance a checkbook—but nevertheless I took the leap. I started Girls Dreaming Big in January of 2013, while continuing to teach full time.

I can't say I was an amazing teacher that semester, but it was great for my business and collecting what I now know is called "qualitative market research." I spent countless hours talking to the young women in my math classes to find out what they needed and wanted. I listened carefully and shaped my entire business around their feedback: what young women with incredible potential want and need, and perhaps most importantly, how to engage them.

I got off to a strong start. Right out of the gate, I was featured on Sheryl Sandberg's LeanIn.org site, held a successful mother-daughter workshop, took a group of six young women on a Personal Growth Trip to Bali, and had a growing client list for coaching and tutoring. This was starting to look, feel, and become a real business and my confidence was rising.

And so at the end of the 2012-13 school year, I left teaching to focus on my company full time. I assumed I would be much more productive without a teaching career getting in my way. Look at all I had accomplished while I was working! Surely I can do even more once I had more time!

Boy was I *wrong*!!!

I never realized how much of a role my classroom, going into work every day, and having my peers around me to give me an, "'Atta girl!" was playing into my early success.

This brings me back to my favorite painting, *A Sunday Afternoon*. I'm drawn to it for more than just my fascination with the art form of pointillism. I love that it conveys such a strong sense of community and connection.

When I left teaching, I floundered because community and connection were lacking in my life. I felt incredibly isolated and alone as I bounced between my home "office" (aka—my couch), the library, and local cafes. The worst part was it made me start to question my decision to go after my dreams.

As I reflected (or at times wallowed in my loneliness), I realized that although technology has helped us become more connected than ever before, we're actually quite disconnected. Think about it: you don't even have to leave your house to buy groceries anymore. While I can appreciate this luxury on a cold winter day, these "conveniences" are actually doing us a huge disservice.

Humans are hardwired for connection and when it's lacking, it not only has an emotional impact, but a physical one, too. Research shows that a lack of social connection is as bad for our health as smoking *15 cigarettes a day*.

And it's not just about our personal well being. The Kauffman Foundation found one of the most significant predictors of a business owner's success is their social capital. Sadly, many studies suggest that women have less or different access to social capital, but according to the same studies, women rank social support and encouragement as the highest on their list of needs.

As a result of all this, what I had been feeling, and my hidden serial entrepreneur side, I decided to start a second company: RISE Collaborative Workspace. I wanted to create a home not only for the teen girls I worked with through Girls Dreaming Big, but also for the amazing business women I had connected with along my journey who were searching for the same things I was.

I wish I could tell you it was an easy process from idea to execution, but it was far from it. I had so many days when I wanted to quit or thought it was never going to happen. What kept me going was when I met with impressive women who would get excited by what I was trying to create and ask me how they could help.

I got to live out the vision of RISE Collaborative Workspace. Through the collaboration and support of countless women and men, I was able to RISE up and make my dream a reality. And that's when I knew these dots on the page were turning into something big.

All along the way, I've said, "I don't want to get to the top by myself. I want to be surrounded by my friends." And with this business, I am incredibly lucky that is coming true. I am surrounded by some of the most strong, smart, and successful women (many of whom you will read about in the chapters that follow) and RISE Collaborative is truly only a reality today because of the endless support, help, and encouragement those women provided me. The best part is I now get to go to work every day and be surrounded by them!

While so many of my "dots" felt incredibly random and misplaced, I can now see how every step or point I made has come together to make a beautiful painting: one that depicts a gathering of ambitious women supporting one another and achieving goals they never thought they would reach. And I'm one of the many faces in that crowd.

As the Founder/CEO of RISE Collaborative, Stacy Taubman launched a company that is changing the way women do business. RISE Collaborative Workspace has been featured in publications including *USA Today, Bloomberg, St. Louis Business Journal,* and *ELLE Magazine* as a leader in the multi-billion-dollar coworking industry. Since opening in early 2017, RISE Collaborative's growing membership includes close to 200 of some of the most impressive businesswomen in St. Louis. Dozens of members have reported business growth of 200% or more since joining RISE Collaborative, a true testament to the impact investing in women can have. Focused on empowering women in business and building social capital, Stacy and RISE Collaborative create meaningful connections between individuals, companies and organizations to foster a stronger and healthier business community for women in St. Louis.

Continued

Stacy Taubman
stacy@riseworkspace.com
RISEworkspace.com

Facebook: facebook.com/RISECollaborativeWorkspace
Twitter: twitter.com/RISEcollabwkspc
Linkedin: linkedin/in/StacyTaubman
Instagram: instagram.com/RISECollaborativeWorkspace

The Road Map

When I got my driver's license, the first thing my mother gave me was a folded paper road map. "You need a map handy in case you get lost so you can find your way," she told me.

Even in the pre-smartphone era, the map felt incredibly uncool, and I begrudgingly stuffed it in my glove compartment. However, having the map was surprisingly reassuring; we're taught that getting lost makes us vulnerable... it's scary... dangerous, even. Having a piece of paper to keep me safe might not have been the worst idea, even coming from a mother to her teenage daughter.

As the years went by, I began to find road maps stuffed in other "glove compartments." In college, a step-by-step course list led me to the graduation stage. Emily Post guided me through the who, what, when, and how of planning the perfect wedding. And in the workplace, an engrained hierarchy of titles, positions, and salary ranges comfortably told me where I ranked and where I needed to go if I wanted to get to the top.

As a Type A, firstborn overachiever, of course I wanted to get to the top! If you don't win, you're a loser, right? And so I unfurled that career road map and stepped right in.

There's something very comforting about having rules and a plan. It provides constant reassurance you're doing the right thing, and sublime satisfaction and success will be waiting for you after each turn. A promotion—hooray! A ten-percent bonus—you did it! People reporting directly to you, more meetings to attend with fellow bigwigs, and "Senior" added to the front of your title! My goodness, these must have been the things the Pilgrims' dreams were made of!

And it did feel good. Achievement and pleasing others had been my drugs for decades and there was no better setting for me to get my high than in corporate America.

But like any drug, there comes a hangover. Sometimes, you need an intervention.

My rock bottom came after a decade working in public relations and marketing. Agency life suited me well. It came with a reassuring pecking order of titles and a seemingly endless stream of reports, tasks, meetings, and emails arriving rapid-fire twenty-four-seven, 365 days a year to make you feel like you were saving lives as you drafted ad copy, press releases, and speeches for your clients.

There were also plenty of young, catty millennial colleagues with sharp elbows with whom to commiserate over the long hours and "awful management" (one of the corporate worker bee's favorite drugs), then use that data against you as soon as you turned your back.

Yet I was right where I thought I wanted to be. Where I was supposed to be. Where the road map took me.

On New Year's Eve 2013, my husband confided that he was worried about me, and 2014 was the time for a change. It wasn't all of the late nights or the vacations stolen by work emails. It wasn't the frustration with my bosses or the catty colleagues. It was something I had said days prior that he couldn't get out of his head.

"I make money for other people by making other people feel less-than," I'd said to him off-handedly.

Marketing is a business of telling people what they're missing. The products and services they don't have and need more of, or that everyone else wants and so should they. And that need for more, better, and now is all part of the American Dream Road Map. Buy this, do that, follow the Yellow Brick Road and you'll be happy, happy, happy!

But for me, I wasn't getting happier. My husband could sense that and wanted more for himself, too, as he was also exhausted and empty from chasing paychecks. And so that night, we took a U-turn: we decided to leave our jobs and move across the country with a trip to Europe in-between (because when you're homeless and unemployed, you might as well head to Europe!)

We were both ready for more. More fulfillment. More family. More of what really matters—at least to us.

While in Europe, I wrote a lot. I spent a lot of time in still-ness and reflection. I ate, and explored, and read, and talked with strangers about their lives, as I figured out what I wanted for mine. It was the best detour I've ever taken.

When we returned to the United States and settled into our new/old home of St. Louis, I had big plans and even bigger dreams. I was confident in my new direction: I'd leave the corporate world behind for good and work for myself. I'd do the work I loved for the clients I believed in and I'd change their futures and mine for the better by sharing their stories and lifting us all up, because a rising tide lifts all boats!

And then my boat sank.

Because, you see, there is no road map for the wanderer. I was taking a new path using a broken compass I didn't know how to read, and I quickly got lost. I had come to depend on my map and didn't know how to forge a new path alone. And I felt so alone.

The long days while my husband was at work were suffocat-ing. Sitting alone in my home office, the silence was deafening. Gathering my things to work from a coffee shop was fun at first, but somehow being surrounded by so many strangers had never felt so isolating.

I never realized how much I needed the company of others along my journey. The ideas, the camaraderie, the encouragement, and accountability. Heck, people to get dressed up for! Like Dor-othy, I needed my people as I skipped along in my ruby slippers.

Then one day, my people found me. Networking events can often feel akin to a root canal, but for some reason, my compass pulled me into one such event in the spring of 2016. There was free wine so I figured I had nothing to lose! As I sipped my sauvignon blanc and listened to the featured panelists tell their stories, for the first time in a long time, I felt a connection.

An entrepreneur named Stacy Taubman was telling her story—my story—of disconnection in isolation. But the difference was she was doing something about it. She was working to create a place where women could build community, connections, and confidence while they pursued their professional dreams. I needed this place in my life. I wanted to be a member and wanted to do whatever it took to make it a reality.

And just like that, my compass pointed north again and I tossed that road map out the window.

The rest, as they say, is history. I am now Stacy's business partner and the COO of RISE Collaborative Workspace. Every day, I face new challenges, make thousands of decisions I never expected, and do it all in the name of supporting and encouraging other women with big dreams. And I'm no longer doing it alone. We are raising the tide for our members and we are truly watching it lift each and every member's boat. I no longer make people feel less than; I get to help them become more.

This was not on the road map I received when I graduated all those years ago. Shredding my cushy paycheck, tossing out my titles, and pulling off of the corporate freeway was a detour filled with warning signs, flashing lights, and even some barking dogs!

And since it isn't on the map, I have no idea where this new road leads. It may be straight and fast like the autobahn, taking us to entrepreneurial and financial success beyond our wildest dreams. Maybe it's long and winding like a country road, with turns to try and hills to soar along. Or it may connect back to the "safety" of the corporate freeway one day. You never know.

In the meantime, I've got my windows down, a warm breeze in my hair, and a killer playlist going. There's an extra seat open if you want to join in—but no maps or backseat drivers allowed!

Kate Wiegmann is Partner and Chief Operating Officer of RISE Collaborative Workspace, a female-focused business community that provides coworking space and resources to help its members find success both personally and professionally. Prior to helping open RISE Collaborative in 2016, Kate worked in public relations and marketing representing large national brands as well as local businesses, nonprofits, and politicians in her second home of Greenville, South Carolina. A graduate of the University of Missouri School of Journalism, Kate is a skilled storyteller and writer. When she's not passionately supporting St. Louis businesswomen and growing RISE Collaborative, she is a freelance writer, consults in interior design, and volunteers with Big Brothers Big Sisters and St. Louis Children's Hospital.

Continued

Kate Wiegmann
kate@riseworkspace.com
RISEworkspace.com

Facebook: facebook.com/RISECollaborativeWorkspace/
Twitter: twitter.com/RISEcollabwkspc
Linkedin: linkedin.com/in/kate-wiegmann/
Instagram: instagram.com/RISECollaborativeWorkspace

The Courageous Yes

I've always believed there are three types of career women. The first knows exactly the profession she desires, pursues the resources needed to do it, and happily fulfills her purpose. She makes plans, executes them, and enjoys success. I envy this woman.

The second woman isn't sure of her path, but has firm parameters for a satisfying career. She seeks opportunities that keep her close to her interests and appreciates that flexibility can lead to unexpected happiness. These women are my closest friends.

The third woman samples freely from a smorgasbord of professions. She has never been sure of her trajectory, worries she may not fulfill her purpose and wakes up in her forties still wondering what she wants to be when she grows up. Career? It's more like a series of clumsy trips that face-plant into surprisingly great opportunities. I am this woman.

I have been a writer, a fundraiser, a radio personality, a singer, an executive director, a vice president, an event planner, an acting instructor, a leadership trainer, a policy advisor, a candle maker, a diversity consultant, and a CEO. I have worked in nonprofits, corporations, as a sole proprietor, and in government. My career has touched a variety of industries including criminal justice, teen pregnancy, substance abuse, leadership, and organizational development, care of the elderly, crisis response, cancer research, domestic violence, and education (to name a few). It's been colorful, difficult, satisfying, adventurous, and scary. And I have loved every minute of it.

Before I go on sounding like a professional vagabond, let me explain: I love the word "yes." It is full of possibility. I consider only three factors before accepting a new career or volunteer challenge: Will it be interesting? Will it be meaningful, invoking a feeling of purpose? And, most importantly, is it an opportunity to serve others? If the answer to these questions is "yes," I say yes.

I've come to call this the "Courageous Yes." Beyond the easier "yes" that comes with a safe bet, the Courageous Yes asks me to commit despite my fears, shortcomings, or the difficulty ahead. It doesn't accept thoughts that I won't know enough, won't be happy, or won't succeed. It plows through the breathtaking terror of the unknown. It acknowledges with humility that I may be the right person to accomplish a specific objective. The Courageous Yes is challenging, vulnerable, and even occasionally disappointing. And I've never regretted it.

This Yes has led me to working with dozens of nonprofits to make my community a better place. From helping victims find hope after crime and violence, to encouraging others to believe in their strengths, and to providing the strategic and administrative foundation for programs that change our world for the better.

It led me from a life in theater and media to working with the Department of Justice, as an executive director for a Missouri Supreme Court Commission, as a CEO of a social enterprise, and to training hundreds to improve their capacity to serve in leadership positions.

It opened possibilities to serve as the first executive director of a women's foundation, to ensure veterans have access to quality cancer care, and to coaching individuals to identify purpose and fulfillment in their work. And it was a special Courageous Yes that led me to launch Sentient Strategy, a leadership and organizational development firm that develops socially intelligent, innovative leaders.

The Courageous Yes helped me find purpose. I've always been a storyteller of sorts, lending my voice to what I think may help others. I pursued degrees in musical theater and communications because I loved performing. On stage, I used my voice to sing and speak stories of great imagination, stories that conveyed the complexities of the human condition. I helped people escape, connect, cry, and laugh.

But after working in radio, television, and theater, I realized it wasn't being on stage or on air that gave me purpose. It was knowing I have a unique ability to translate intimate and abstract thoughts into shared and accessible language—to be a conduit for emotional connection. It wasn't a job title or industry I was pursuing, it was a purpose. And I was going to have to say yes to new, and possibly scary, opportunities to fulfill that purpose.

My first Courageous Yes was to an opportunity in Kansas City working in fundraising. I knew absolutely nothing about fundraising but was told I would be able to use my voice to inspire donors to help people. The position left me exhausted and frustrated, and in a perpetual state of elation. I had the ability to serve hundreds in need just by telling their story in meaningful ways. It was exciting to find that an entirely different kind of work could be so rewarding, and I planned to stay a while.

Soon, however, a life-changing personal assault would bring me back home to St. Louis. A new, untranslated story now moved around in my mind. The story was my own. I sought to identify with others who could share this new and unwelcomed language. Like a raging river that leads to a stream and eventually to mist, I believed if I could name this experience, if I could give voice to the kind of hope that breaks through grief, perhaps my own grief could evaporate.

I worked various fundraising and communications jobs until I felt strong enough to say my next Courageous Yes. This came when I accepted a position as President and CEO of the Crime Victim Advocacy Center, where I faced a world that swirled with hundreds of stories like mine. During my ten years as CEO, I had the honor of giving voice to thousands who had been silenced by violence, grief, poverty, and systemic inequities. I learned my voice didn't just serve in a way that led others to understanding or empathy. I had the power to use my voice to change circumstances for others.

It took a particularly Courageous Yes to speak up to those in positions of authority to ask for difficult, unpopular and time-consuming change to their way of leading our communities. My voice was often tired and sore. Though there is still much work to be done, I am eternally grateful that others listened. Many lives are better because they did.

During this time, I said a Courageous Yes to other new experiences. To leading the board of directors for a charter school, launching a social enterprise into the unknown field of retail, and working on women's issues. Along the way, I was asked to train women in a leadership development program. I knew nothing about this type of training, how this opportunity would fit into my life, or how I would be received by the participants. I was truly terrified—and deeply interested. The Courageous Yes requires fearlessness. And it always leads to purpose and satisfaction.

It didn't take long for me to realize this work catapulted my purpose. I translated women's fears and vulnerabilities into a reflection of their strengths and possibilities. I encouraged them to say their own Courageous Yes. I helped them navigate critical work situations and discover how to integrate their personal passion into their profession. I conveyed stories that helped them understand how to make a meaningful impact in their community. This work was deeply satisfying, and is the reason I started my company.

Today I help professionals solve complex personal and organizational problems with skills I amassed because I said yes to new and challenging opportunities. I have the privilege of dabbling across sectors to discover and catapult the unique strengths of amazing individuals, companies, and communities worldwide. I am grateful and happy.

I would have missed incredible experiences, joy, and accomplishments had I not embraced the Courageous Yes. Because I did, I spend every day playing a part in helping the human spirit exceed itself. And that is the greatest YES of all.

Julie Lawson is a leadership consultant, speaker, nonprofit executive and champion of women's success. She has trained and coached hundreds of women leaders and consulted for several nonprofits to build leadership strategies that meets the needs of a changing community. She believes deeply in the power of the collective human spirit.

She is certified in change management, executive coaching, crisis response, terrorism victimization, cultural competency and a variety of leadership methodologies. With degrees in Theater, Media, Organizational Communications & Psychology and post-graduate work in Leadership Methodology, she never shies from pursuing a wide range of interests.

Julie's passion is helping leaders and organizations discover and maximize their strengths, particularly when focused on solving community issues. She also remains a dedicated warrior for victims of violence and human trafficking and considers helping victims an important theme in her life's work. In 2017 she founded Sentient Strategy where she helps nonprofits and leaders access

Continued

their full potential and develop business strategies that reflect their integrity and purpose. Her work includes serving as Executive Director of Connected Learning (St. Louis) and the Association of VA Hematology/Oncology, and as the inaugural Executive Director of RISE Society (www.risesocietystl.org).

In her spare time, she volunteers for a variety of organizations (she can't stop saying yes to a meaningful cause!), enjoys writing, is an avid reader, and sings at special events.

Julie Lawson
314-853-6063
jlawson@sentient-strategy.com
sentient-strategy.com; juliehlawson.com

Facebook: facebook.com/jhlawson
Twitter: twitter.com/juliehlawson
LinkedIn: linkedin.com/in/julielawson

Where I'm Going

I had just fired my therapist, I was still fifty pounds heavier than eighteen months prior, I couldn't remember the last time I wore pants that zipped, and the thought of going to work made me physically nauseous.

How did I get here?

It was March 7, 2011. I was walking into a weekly manager's meeting at my company's headquarters around 7:30 A.M. when my mom called. She said I needed to get to the hospital.

By the time my sister and I were able to meet my mom and see my dad, he was on a morphine drip. He was unresponsive when the ambulance picked him up that morning, and he remained unresponsiveness through the many room and nurse changes throughout that day.

Late in the evening, we were assigned a hospice nurse. During one visit, she dropped off snacks, asked how we were, and if we needed anything. I remember looking for her when I stepped outside of my dad's room later. She was near the elevator, and when I started to speak with her, she glanced at her watch, told me her shift was over, and quickly hopped on. It seemed like she was trying to avoid sharing the news we didn't want to hear.

My dad passed away around ten-thirty that night. The machines did everything you see in the movies—the beeping, the flat line, and the lights. What I didn't know from the movies, was that in a split second before my dad would pass away I would feel a part of my heart and soul disappear.

The better part of the year leading up to March 7 had been a combination of good days and bad days, lots of trips to the hospital, and not enough family time. I watched my dad grow weaker physically, but never mentally or emotionally. Throughout his diagnosis, he kept his sense of humor, his resilience, and his ability to take care of us.

I left my corporate job shortly after I learned he had cancer and joined a family-owned company. I thought the work-life balance would be better in case his health went downhill. I was relieved with the flexibility to go to the hospital when needed, take phone calls as they came in, and not have to organize my stapler before leaving if I had to rush out.

I started seeing a therapist, convincing myself that somehow she would have answers to questions I hadn't even thought of.

After my dad passed away, nurses quickly came in asking us if we had made arrangements, telling us we had a limited amount of time to do so. The next few weeks and months were a blur.

After a week of crying, drinking, planning a wake and a funeral, I wanted things back to normal. I remember asking a co-worker to throw away any cards or flowers that were in my office before I got back. I assured her I would be fine when I came back as long as no one asked me if I was okay.

During one of my first weeks back, a colleague walked into a full conference room, finger guns blazing, and proudly stated, "I finally got to see Kate cry!"

I was stunned. Of course she had—at my father's wake. I stared at her blankly. She laughed. Quickly, everyone else joined in, laughing with her and joking about my "weakness."

At that moment, I realized all the awards, the best places to work recognition, the company picnics, the work perks, the family-first benefits, all of it—they weren't real, they were all marketing ploys. Sure, they were real in the sense that we had a picnic, we had vacation days, we had the plaques on the wall, but they weren't authentic.

The job that I loved because of its promised culture was a fraud.

Over the course of the months following my dad's death, I lost the excitement I once had to go to work every day. I was no longer the first one in or the last one out. I went from giving 120 percent every day to about 90 percent. My boss and I no longer had our 7 A.M. calls. I knew he was ready for me to "get back to normal."

The problem was, I couldn't go back. Trauma and grief have a funny way of changing you in ways you don't expect and can't explain. I knew he and I had to come to an understanding on this. I didn't know how to tell him this was normal. I'm not sure I knew it myself at the time. We never had a conversation about it, because I quit.

I knew I couldn't put into words what I needed, and my company had shown they didn't know either. A little over a year after my dad's death, I gave my notice and my boss told me to leave that Friday afternoon.

I didn't actually have a plan, but for the first time in months I felt relieved. I no longer had the energy to "be okay" for eight-plus hours a day, and I knew come Monday I wouldn't have to try. I wasn't sure if I was on my way to or from rock bottom. I couldn't remember the week of my dad's funeral or how many months had passed since returning to work, but I finally slept.

I spent almost a year out of work. During that time, I realized a lot about self-care, relationships, and work culture that I wish I had known before my dad was diagnosed. Although, I'm not sure knowing it would have helped at the time.

I started working out regularly again, with a goal of getting back into shape before going to back to work. I was eating healthier, sleeping better, and working out on schedule. My self-care routine eventually led me to holistic medicine alternatives. This helped me make the decision to become a certified yoga instructor with the desire to use yoga as a way to give back.

Several of my relationships took a hit during the time my dad was sick, and in the months and years after his death. I can't say I blame those who opted to end our relationship.

I wasn't the most attractive dating prospect at the time. I always truly believed the best part of marrying me would be the father-in-law my husband would have. Shortly after my dad's passing, I decided I never wanted to marry. My therapist would tell you this was my safety net to avoid a relationship where I could again experience loss.

Some friends gave up on me pretty quickly, realizing that I wasn't as much fun as I used to be, and others slowly slipped out of my life once they realized things weren't going back to the way they were.

My friends that stayed around, and those who I met after my dad's death, are truly some of the strongest and most graceful people I know. They are the ones who still come over when I can't sleep, spend every anniversary with me, and let me cry at midnight. They are the ones who accept me, knowing that I won't be okay every single day and that's alright.

In reflecting on the past two years, I realize I had been a pretty crappy friend. Had I known then what I know now, I doubt much would have changed. I wasn't in a position emotionally or mentally to be the better friend. I'm hopeful that when I have friends on the other side, I'll be a strong enough friend to be there for them when they are ready.

I realized work relationships weren't as strong as they seemed, and was more often than not contingent on a mutual benefit that no longer existed once I left. This was a mix of sadness, disappointment, and relief. I was sad to lose people who I thought were so close to me, and disappointed that the work-life balance and family culture I bought into wasn't a reality in the end. I was also relieved that I was able to stop investing in people who weren't invested in me.

Finally, I had plenty of time to reflect on work culture. I didn't want to go back to a place that made me unhappy or that made others unhappy. When I decided to start looking for jobs, I turned down more interviews than I accepted.

Despite receiving advice to hide my time out of work, I chose to be very open with potential employers as a way to find the work-life balance and culture I now knew I needed. Finding a professional home and a boss who was supportive of professional and personal endeavors proved to be the right choice. Now that I've moved on, I know I made the best choice—my relationships with past co-workers are just as strong as when I was a co-worker.

Since then, it's been my hope as a leader and co-worker to better recognize when outside influences may be affecting someone at work, to offer support, and to always make sure the office is a place they want to be.

Now that I've shared how I got here, it's time to figure out where I'm going.

Kate Ewing is a results-oriented strategic marketing professional. She currently serves as the Director of Marketing for Mueller Prost CPAs + Business Advisors, where her primary focus is to drive business results through developing and implementing marketing, communications, and business development strategies for the firm. Kate also directs media relations, branding, advertising, social media, and web development and oversees sponsorships and contributions. In addition, Ewing is an adjunct marketing professor for Lindenwood University and Webster University.

After losing her father in 2011, Kate's focus shifted to finding and cultivating positive workplace cultures and implementing self care into the work week. As a certified yoga instructor, Kate strives to take her practice from the mat to the office daily. Outside of work, Kate serves on several local charitable boards and committees, with an emphasis on cancer research funding, arts and education, and re-entry services. She also mentors female entrepreneurs in several areas including securing funding, creating business plans and implementing marketing strategies.

Continued

Kate is a St. Louis native who currently lives in St. Louis' Tower Grove East neighborhood with her rescue cats, and is aunt to her sister's kids, Aiden and Zoey.

Kate Ewing
kate.d.ewing@gmail.com

Twitter: twitter.com/kathryn_ewing
Linkedin: linkedin.com/in/kateewing/

From Place to Position

"Sometimes the smallest step in the right direction ends up being the biggest step of your life.

Tiptoe if you must, but take the first step."

– Naeem Callaway

Over the past year, many, if not all conversations I have had centered on transition, change, and shift. To be transparent, during the same time, my personal and professional lives were also saturated with transition, change, and shift. I had found myself in this very interesting, unsettling space. To unpack this more, I was a little anxious and there was this bubbling feeling of anticipation deep in my belly. I've never delivered a child, but those feelings mimicked what little I knew about a pregnant woman right before giving birth. Not the pain, but the need to push.

This overwhelming feeling within was a nudge of urgency to push past my fears, doubts, and insecurities into unknown deep waters and new territory. The sphere where I would operate in— one in which I knew I had been placed on earth to do—was a domain where passion and compassion ruled my efforts. When in this space, I would give of myself, talents, and gifts to make this world better. Today, I get tickled when I reflect on that organized vision that was trapped in my grand imagination. It wasn't that the dream couldn't become a reality; the roadblock was me, myself, and I. I was the barrier between reality and what seemed impossible. It was in this period I exposed the fact that I was in place, not position.

In talking with mentors and those more seasoned in life, I discovered that this battle with insecurity and feeling ill-equipped is normal during transformative seasons. Growing up, my parents would tell me, "If you can think it, you can be it; if you can see it, you can have it, BUT you must put in the work." I discovered finding my rhythm to put in the work was the key to living a fruitful life, my best life.

Now in my adult life, I realize part of putting in the work consists of many factors. One key concept is moving from place to position. The dictionary defines place as cause to be in a particular point, area, or situation; an available seat or accommodation; a vacancy. Position is defined as a situation or set of circumstances, especially one that affects one's power to act; a person's particular point of view or attitude toward something; the location where someone or something should be; the correct place.

My interpretation of being in place means holding a spot, taking up the space while waiting to be moved; the need to ask for permission or be permitted to move, act, do, or say. At different points in life, we all have and will find ourselves in place—a spot in which we know we're kind of existing just to fill a vacant spot. The issue is, far too many of us have fallen asleep in place. It is here that we can lose the fortitude to push past barriers and challenges of life. It's here that many exchange their optimism for idleness. Being in place allows you to show up but not have impact. Being in place provides the chance to dream but not pursue. It tells that one has surrendered to default living.

My clarification of being in position suggests operating with courage to do and be without apology or permission; having the nerve to serve in truth; and operating in purpose, on purpose while impacting lives outside of self. Someone who's in position shows up with contagious confidence others attempt to mirror. This person does not flee vulnerability. This person has pride by standing in their truth. S/He is always learning as much as they teach, giving as much as they collect. Being in position suggests an ability to influence an atmosphere just by being present. A positioned person has lips that not only share information but also impartation. It allows one to lead without a title. It communicates the individual functions with intentionality and purpose. They acknowledge they have imperfections, but realize this is part of being human and make every mistake into a personal learning experience. Fear is embraced and used to propel the vision.

My lifestyle and accomplishments screamed an indisputable fruitful life. I and those around me had no doubt I was living my best life. But what I was ignoring, and others turned a blind eye to, was the malnutrition of unfulfillment. Yes, I was producing great things and showing up in great places. What I didn't realize is that I was putting in the wrong work in the wrong space that didn't even align with the desires of my heart. I struggled to maintain my reoccurring performance in this drama series, but that bubbling within the pit of my belly intensely rumbled. I fought it by trying to live in a comfortable place. One day it overcame me. I could no longer fight. The day I surrendered, I moved into position.

I tapped into a buried dwelling of confidence to push past self and a place of familiar comfort to get in position. It wasn't easy, but I pushed. How liberating it is to answer a life's call! I terminated my past successes by leaving an established career, ending board of director memberships, concluding volunteer roles, and even releasing some relationships. Make a note that these things and people were good but not good for where I was headed. With all of these changes I realized being in position was more than a physical location. It also included my head, heart, and hands.

Head Position
Clarity, Interpretation, Knowledge, Vision

Heart Position
Grit, Desire, Passion, Resolve

Hand Position
Act, Build, Collect, Serve

Mindset matters. Before anything happens in our lives—personally and/or professionally—thought must occur. Dominating thoughts have direct impact on the outcomes of life. Once I shared with others that I would be stepping down from my senior-level role into a start-up nonprofit, my spirit was trampled by negative insight, doubt, and intrusive questions. Had I not had clarity and belief in what I wanted for my life, I would have crumbled or remained in that unfulfilling, good-paying place. I had and continue to manage my head position by feeding my mind positive declarations. I stopped being my own worst enemy by not seeking approval or validation, stopped the comparisons, ceased the worrying, and scheduled downtime.

Following the heart serves as a guiding truth to take risks and push past self-imposed limitations. I realized that I first had to mend my heart and forgive myself. After years of dimming my own light, some restoration needed to occur. Next, I needed to unlock my passion. Confidence and grit strengthened when I began to make honest decisions, set up systems of accountability, move past failure, and visualize outcomes. These acts called for daily discipline; they were/are not one-and-done actions. Operating with heart position proved to power both my new victories and my willingness to consider and inspire others.

I had to shake hands and initiate new relationships with individuals from diverse backgrounds while nurturing former acquaintances. I had to raise hands and ask for help and resources from individuals and groups that had to be educated of my needs and passion. I had to extend hands and offer my assistance when needed. Knowing actions spoke louder than words, I had to push past being timid to exercise my hand position. This is the area in which I could have self-selected to abort the journey, but I learned to be comfortable being uncomfortable. I had to take action—not wait for action to find me—even when it didn't make sense to others or myself.

For me, getting out of place and into position was and continues to be a process. A daily commitment to discipline myself to operate with vision, clarity, and actions has elevated my life from unsatisfied to fruitful. No longer am I dismayed by my own limited thoughts, self-doubt, and fear of taking risks. That bubbling feeling within me settled once I pushed past the "stuff." Putting in the work has taken me off the sidelines of life and into the game. What's interesting: I thought I had been living a life of delight and wonder; however, this joy and contentment I have today is worth more than accolades, silver, or gold. When the next nudge of urgency visits, I won't ignore it. I will position my head, heart, and hands to respond, understanding I can't do one without the other.

There's no doubt I will continue to be engaged in conversations of transition, change, and shift. Moving forward, I will share my revelations and declare that no matter the pace, a decision to move from taking up space into courageous purpose must be completed. Despite the circumstances, pushing from place to position is truly the practice to live your best life.

As an advocate for inclusion and leadership development, Nicci Roach has been fortunate to partner with individuals, community leaders, academic institutions and organizations—both domestic and international. For more than 15 years, Nicci has served as a change agent, stimulating the inclusion of underrepresented populations while equipping advancing leaders. She currently serves as Webster University's inaugural Associate Vice President for Diversity and Inclusion and Senior Director for Community Engagement. As an adjunct faculty member, she teaches courses in leadership and organizational development.

Nicci is also the Co-Founder and Chief Operating Officer of Mosaic Ceiling, whose mission is, "Empowering Women One Ceiling at a Time." Through diverse programming, individuals and groups are educated and equipped with strategies to help women advance while breaking down barriers.

Nicci holds a Master of Arts in Public Relations; Master of Arts in Human Resources; and a Bachelor of Arts in Media Communi-

Continued

cations with a minor in Women's Studies from Webster University. She has completed two certificate programs, Diversity Management at Cornell University and Women in Educational Leadership at Harvard University. She is currently completing a doctorate in higher education leadership at Missouri Baptist University.

Nicci Roach
314-266-8593
hello@nicciroach.com
nicciroach.com

Facebook: facebook.com/nicci.roach.3
Twitter: twitter.com/NicciRoach
Linkedin: linkedin.com/in/nicciroach/

Rock-Star Friends

Amy and Sara: We know the power in working together and supporting each other, taking lessons learned and using them to pull each other up along the ascent. Most importantly, we all deserve our own group of women to lean on through the ups and downs of life and career. Who doesn't want a rock-star friend in life to lean in with, someone who is always there, supporting us personally and professionally in every way, not only because they want to and can, but because they understand you and what you do? We all want the kind of friendship that makes life's journey more enjoyable, fulfilling, and complete every day. This is what it is like to have a rock-star friend in life.

We met in law school, and together have supported each other by practicing the concept of "leaning in" in every aspect of our lives. Our friendship continued to grow after law school as we navigated working as young lawyers, overcoming struggles in the practice of law and life, celebrating marriages and families, keeping a balance with the pressure and success, and being that person so phenomenal in supporting the other in everything—nothing short of a rock star for the other.

Amy: It was 1998, a hot and humid summer day in August in St. Louis. I was about to start my first year at law school, a three-year journey leading to my legal career. I remember thinking how my life was about to change in so many ways. My life was about to be inundated with new friends, the law, a new way of think-ing, including that scary sounding Socratic Method, and new time management. Frankly, my life would become the job of living and breathing law school. Though I knew this was not going to be easy, I could not fully appreciate the complexity, stress, pressure, and intensity awaiting me. It was in law school that Sara and I met. We became a support system not only in law school, but in our lives that followed.

How would I describe Sara? Simply put, she is fiercely hardworking, kind, outgoing, friendly, loyal, and dedicated. We managed to spend three years learning all about contracts, torts, criminal, and constitutional law. We studied together late into the night—sharing outlines for classes, questioning and preparing one another, laughing, crying, and stressing over passing classes.

Sara: I remember walking into the auditorium for the first time, greeted by a sea of new and eager faces. There was a buzz of excitement and anxiety in the room as we all tried to take in the newness while creating connections.

I am so incredibly grateful that Amy was one of those new connections for me. The support throughout law school and our entire careers has been invaluable. How would I describe Amy? Amy is an incredibly passionate advocate, clever, thoughtful, tough, professional, and devoted to her clients. It has been such a pleasure to watch and be a part of Amy's life and professional development. I have learned so much!

Amy: After three years, I graduated and set off to begin work-ing. Sara, the more ambitious, remained in school to earn an MBA. At my graduation, Sara sat with my father and enthusiastically was present at the ceremony and special dinner to help celebrate this milestone. When Sara graduated the next year, I sat right next to her father at the ceremony, and went out to her special dinner to celebrate her milestone. Our fathers had both been great influences in our lives; we shared that and are both grateful to have had them. This time would begin a new journey for both of us.

After law school, Sara started working for a prestigious downtown St. Louis law firm. She worked in their corporate department, strategizing in the development and formation of companies. We talked about the hard work, long hours, and difficult learning curve awaiting us. Two years into our legal careers, and no surprise to anyone, Sara received the St. Louis Business Journal's prestigious 30 Under 30 award, presented to thirty St. Louisans under age thirty who are on the rise. Sara called, saying, "Would you come for the awards ceremony?"

"Would I? Are you kidding me? I'll be there waving the biggest GO Sara GO sign!" Of course, I planned to go, and I was sort of kidding about the sign. I wanted to shout from the rooftops. Her happiness was my happiness. When a friend succeeds, you want to be there to cheer her on and show her how proud you are. In many ways, I really wasn't kidding about the GO Sara GO! Sign, because it represented a tangible way to measure her accomplishments in such a short time.

Sara: I remember getting the phone call about this award and calling Amy to ask her to be part of my law firm's invited guests and sit at their reserved table at the event. I had a limited number of seats, and invited my partners, family, and Amy. I was excited and nervous to be honored for this award, and was thrilled the people who supported me could be there.

Amy started out at a medium sized firm of twenty-five lawyers as a civil litigator (an attorney who works for individuals and companies spending most of her time in court). Less than two years out of law school, she had her first jury trial. Yes, it was a bit of a daunting experience to put together all of the pieces of legal analysis, trial strategy, and preparation on her own, while she was still in the process of learning and understanding the legal system. The case ultimately settled: Hooray! I remember Amy calling to share the news, and of course we had to celebrate by going out to dinner. I was so thrilled for Amy, and told her so that night—"I'm so proud of you winning this motion and winning this case." It was such an amazing accomplishment at such an early stage of her career, and just the first of many amazing accomplishments along the way.

Amy: I knew exactly who I wanted to tell when I received the news about my case—Sara. I knew she would be as happy for me as I was for myself. We were never competitors; we were always allies. I called Sara knowing she would want to celebrate by going out to dinner. Sara was proud of me and for me. She was my champion; I felt her happiness and joy evidenced through her kind and generous words.

Sara and Amy: As we started garnering more legal experience, contacts, and connections, we both started to grow our desire for what we wanted for our respective law practices. We were both hard at work, with a goal to become equity partners at our firms. In order to achieve these goals, we had a similar list of accomplishments that would have to happen along the way. We both would need to work significant hours, generating business of our own, and completing what other attorneys needed for their cases. We would continue to learn the many practical legal skills not taught in law school, such as managing staff and dealing with difficult lawyers and clients. After having practiced for a period of time and making it through the early years of being a lawyer, we both had our eyes on the partnership prize.

Guess what? We both decided to embark on another journey, marriage and parenthood. Of course, we served as each other's maids of honor, and godmothers to each of our first born, and we could not imagine a better choice for either. Loving children and family, we knew we wanted a full life filled with joy and personal happiness. Neither of us truly understood the reality of parenting and practicing law, but we quickly figured out you could do both.

While our lives changed dramatically after having children and we were adjusting to being new parents, we were still expected to perform at the same capacity, including generating productive hours. We both had our first child several years into our law practice, arriving two months apart. We were able to experience pregnancy not just as women, but as lawyers together. Some things just cannot be planned any better. It broadened our friendship and gave us more things to share and enjoy. We loved it!

Most importantly, we had the opportunity to spend time visiting each other on maternity leave at both the office and at home, bringing much-needed food, sweets, and coffee, or whatever was needed, to one another. We checked in on each other and enjoyed holding babies for each other when we had the chance. We both worried about the impact of this change in and for our lives. Demands came from work and our increasingly busy personal lives. Our roles and responsibilities had increased; this would continue with more children, as well as eventually becoming partners in our respective firms with our even greater goals of running law firms.

We both worked hard to prioritize our families, and often discussed our success in setting limits on working hours (or trying to), while we exchanged helpful hints in order to be more productive. We often talked about the need to access more resources to maximize time with our families. We compared notes about planning ahead at work so we could meet those duties. We worked hard to remind the other it was okay to prioritize ourselves from time-to-time, and to include time for exercise (yoga for Sara, Pilates for Amy), reading for pleasure, music and concerts, travel, including our annual girls' trip, self-care (massage or facial), or grabbing coffee, lunch, or a drink.

After seven or eight years working as lawyers, we both made partner. There was relief and elation. It had been a multi-year journey to arrive at this point. We celebrated the accomplishments of both of us. We had made it through ten-plus years of billable hours and could focus on even bigger goals.

We did not stop there. We both became focused on doing more than just our job. We wanted to change not only the legal world, we wanted to do more for our community. We both felt the desire to help kids, adults, and others who could not afford legal services. We both worked at various times, and in different ways, for a variety of different charities including St. Louis Young Variety,

Legal Services of Eastern Missouri, Urban Future, St. Louis Children's Hospital Development Board The Sheldon, Food Outreach, and the YWCA. We support each other by always attending events for the other, and helping the other raise money and support for each of our charitable interests.

We celebrated when we both won (a few years apart) the Missouri Lawyer's Weekly Women's Justice Award for hard work in the legal field and the community.

Supporting each other came at times when personal and professional help were often much-needed. Sometimes, you just need a friend to affirm that your choices are good ones, even if you believe them to be good choices. We believe that as lawyers, mothers, dominate Type A's, not only did we both have similar goals in work and life, but we understood each other in ways that many others could not. We shared ambition and determination, concerns and fears. We could be strong with the other, and we also could be vulnerable when we needed to be, knowing the other would be there to support us without judgment.

We make it a priority to see each other weekly for coffee, lunch, at a kid event, professional or networking event, or at a dinner, despite overwhelming schedules. Rarely does a day go by that we have not checked in on the other just to see how we are doing via text, email, phone, or visit. We send cards and flowers and messages to the other just because those actions are meaningful. We make it a priority to also celebrate the new accomplishments from a new board membership, to a new client, or success in a case, success in our family life, or even a personal success like running a marathon or flying her first airplane trip solo (hint: it was not Amy).

We also make it a life choice to have our children together for as many events as possible: swimming, ice skating, dinner, a play, a party. How incredible that our three girls and two boys of similar ages love the friendship they have developed on their own? We can only hope our children can have the same kind of friendship we have so lovingly cultivated.

We know, understand, and agree about the need to show up. For us, our actions in being and continuing to be present are what support and nourish our friendship.

Amy: When my father passed away in 2016, just before his passing, Sara surprised me and made the two-hundred-mile round trip to see my father and me. It turned out to be on the day of his passing. When Sara's grandmother passed away and she was pregnant, I traveled to see Sara and her family for the visitation. It was just important for both of us to be there for the other. When Sara started her new law practice, Stock Legal, she invited me to see the new building and space before decorations, paint, and moving in. My husband, Andrew and I, came over to the new building late one Sunday night after that to help move boxes, coordinate moving, bring food, and help in any way possible.

Amy and Sara: Words cannot express the true meaning of someone else giving their time to you when life, children and other priorities are factored in. We both lovingly offer our energy and effort when we need it the most. It's a given. We do the same for each other—no questions asked. In those times when we most need our friends, regardless of the convenience of life and moments, nothing stops us from being part of one another's world.

Even more than showing up, our friendship is such that we both want and need support while navigating crucial decisions about our life as lawyers, as women, and with family. There is no decision, or change in life that is not known, supported, or vetted by the other. We share an ability to be a sounding board for the other, about partnership, difficult issues with practice, child-related issues, or difficulties and life. We are honest and open about our thoughts with the other even if it may be tough to hear. We are respectful and mindful, but have learned how to talk to and with the other. This was particularly important as it relates to our careers as lawyers.

We call each other rock stars. How lucky we are to be one another's rock stars! What we found in each other was a true force; a friendship and support system beyond what we knew or understood in law school. As women on the rise for the last twenty years, we have found success within our own lives while leaning in and supporting and sharing each other's life.

Our journey will continue to be intertwined as we move forward in ever expanding ways both personally as godparents, and professionally as collaborators and cheerleaders for the other. Celebrating and staying dedicated to ourselves, one another and our friendship, knowing the other has changed our lives forever. The first twenty years were fantastic; we cannot wait to lean in for the next twenty, forty, and even more!

We encourage each and every one of you—Go find your rock star, whoever that may be and hold on tight to each other for one incredible journey!

Amy Hoch Hogenson is an attorney and partner at Paule, Camazine and Blumenthal. Amy works exclusively in the area of family law including divorce (including high conflict custody cases), post-divorce enforcement, adoption, paternity, grandparents rights, and prenuptial agreements. In addition to her private practice, Amy also volunteers as a "special private prosecutor" for the domestic violence court in St. Louis County and attorney for Legal Services of Eastern Missouri.

Amy is a graduate of St. Louis University School of Law, where she served as Managing Editor of the St. Louis University Public Law Review and Captain of the Jessup Moot Court team. Amy currently serves on the Board of the Sheldon and Food Outreach. She is involved as a Fundraising Committee Member for Caring for Kids, and a previous board member for Urban Future. Amy is the recipient of the 2012 Women's Justice Award for Rising Star and Super Lawyers Rising Star award for 2009, 2014, 2015, 2016 and 2017.

Continued

Amy resides in University City with her husband, Andrew and two children Alex and Abigail.

Amy Hoch Hogenson
ahogenson@pcblawfirm.com
pcblawfirm.com

Sara Stock's dynamic practice focuses on general corporate work for small to medium sized businesses and commercial real estate transactions. Sara advises her clients in all aspects of the business lifecycle. Sara also assists clients in acquiring, divesting, leasing, financing, and developing commercial real estate. Sara's joint MBA and law degree uniquely position her to provide the highest quality legal advice seasoned with a solid understanding of her clients' business objectives.

Continued

Sara left an equity position at a large St. Louis law firm to join KWS Law, and later to form Stock Legal, because she felt she could better serve her target clients, small- to medium-sized businesses, from a small- to medium-sized law firm. Sara's mom and dad ran the family trucking company out of their home while Sara was a child, and Sara's dad and brother continue to run this successful business today. Sara's husband Steve (with Sara's help) opened a closed-door pharmacy in 2007, which has grown into a thriving company.

Sara is the co-chair of the American Bar Association's Emerging Companies Sub-Committee (Middle Market and Small Business Committee), and sits on the YWCA Board of Directors. Sara is also an active member of ACG St. Louis, and sits on the advisory board for a number of institutions, including banking organizations and local companies.

Sara Stock
314-297-0855
sara.stock@stocklegal.com
stocklegal.com

Facebook: facebook.com/StockLegal/
Linkedin: linkedin.com/company/16155328/
YouTube: youtube.com/channel/UCc5BT2ts09Jeb8Imj1SGIIQ/
featured

Growth Above 14,000 Feet

I t was August in the year 2000. Al Gore and George W. Bush
were running for president of the United States. It was the beginning of reality television with the first year of Survivor. Five of us
went to Africa for three weeks—five women.

The first week of our trip was dedicated to climbing the
mountain in Tanzania, Mount Kilimanjaro. The five of us were out-
fitted with gear for the trek. We had backpacks, Camelbaks, layers
of clothing, boots, snacks, mosquito repellent, sunscreen, tents,
and sleeping bags.

We had each prepared for the climb, but there was a spectrum of ability and readiness in our group. I was in the middle of
the pack, between two women who had trained much more than
me and two that had trained less.

Before we started off the first day, we had a safety meeting. It
included the importance of hydration and the symptoms of high
altitude sickness, including pulmonary and cerebral edema, which
are the most serious and life-threatening illnesses at high altitude.
These are typically risks above 15,000 feet. Our guides told us
just to remember one thing, "Pole, pole." "Pole" means "slowly"
in Swahili. They shared this because it is best to go slower than

normal to allow for more breathing and acclimatization and to mitigate the effects of high altitude.

As we began the trek, three of us soon realized that "pole, pole" really was not going to be a problem for us. You see, the two that were the least conditioned were slower than the two that were the most conditioned. Initially, "pole, pole" was a surprisingly slow pace for some of us.

I recall being the last group to camp every night. We were the last group to eat. We were the last group to go to bed. "Pole, pole" was hard on us. As the days moved on, keeping the slow pace got a little easier. We noticed more about the world around us. Flowers in the high plains desert area had more beauty, and we talked more to one another. We embraced "pole, pole."

When I signed up for the trip, I believe I was mostly focused on reaching the summit of Kilimanjaro. I had not thought much about the journey of the climb, or the time spent on the mountain. As it turned out, we were not only the last to camp at night, but we were frequently the first to leave camp in the morning. We did this intentionally, to extend our day.

This long day of activity on the mountain, especially when we journeyed across the width of the mountain, maintaining an elevation over 14,000 feet for a few days to acclimatize, gave us an advantage. We were climbing the mountain together, and we were cultivating a collective resilience during our climb. In the middle of the climb, we moved from a collapsed volcanic crater that formed the Shira Plateau through a dusty, rocky area that looked like the moon, to a camp called the Lava Tower. Because we were up early and out late, we had the opportunity to engage with all the other groups that were climbing.

Every day, we would interact with other groups as they walked with us and eventually moved past us. We climbed the mountain with people from Great Britain, with people from Texas, with folks from Arkansas, and we walked and talked with our guides. "Pole, pole" gave us the pause in our lives that we needed to learn about each other. This advantage of experiencing the whole climb by extending each day to its fullest...began to pay off.

On the last day of the climb, it was midnight and pitch black, and we had headlamps. We slowly climbed up a rocky ridge in a straight line. It was steep, moving from 15,000 feet toward the summit of over 19,000 feet. The air was thin, and we had to stop A LOT, because at least one person was out of breath. Others were freezing cold. We were wiggling our toes to keep them from being numb in the cold of the night.

We stayed together. We stayed together even when it was hard to maintain a slow pace in the middle of the night, in the cold air. Four women made it to Stella Point in the morning (18,652 ft.), where we lingered for quite a while and looked across the landscape of Africa.

We could see the curvature of the earth in the morning light from that view. We soaked it in and took a "pole, pole" approach at the false summit together. Two moved on and made it to Uhuru Peak, the summit (19,341 ft.), and then returned to camp Barafu to descend together.

What I remember most about this experience of the first week of our journey in Tanzania is the collective resilience that was developed among our five women. This has stayed with me for what is now eighteen years since the trip. Not only do I have lifelong friendships, but I also learned the real power of women is revealed in togetherness, and within the sanctuary of space and time I now call "over 14,000 feet." Growth over 14,000 feet is slow, but it is oh so rich.

This lesson of "pole, pole" has been relearned throughout my life and career as I have navigated being a female brewer in the beer industry. It was also relearned when I became a mother and a stepmother. It was especially evident during times in my life where I have struggled at work or in relationships, when I found sanctuary in the company of women who guided me through tough times and walked slowly with me when it seemed I had lost my way.

This company of women has walked with me when I was not maintaining life's harried pace, and they slowed me down when I was trying to move too fast at "high altitude." These women celebrated with me when I had the big wins in my life, cried with me when I had the big losses, and they gently guided me when I was acting out of my own character. The community of women around me has been my sanctuary, a safe place where I can explore my creativity, without the risk of losing their sacred kinship.

I am grateful for the presence of these friends in my abundant life, and I am honored to be present to cheer them on and walk with them in their own journeys. I am honored to support them when the days are long, the roads are rocky, and the achievements are not in sight. I am privileged to love them through their biggest mistakes.

Now, as an entrepreneur and a seminary student, I try my best to remember "pole, pole." Sometimes I forget, but the reminder of the risks of moving too fast above 14,000 feet creeps back into my memory. Dreams do not have expiration dates, and all great things happen when given enough time and focus.

As a mother, a spouse, and a friend, I have had incredible opportunities to love often and to love big. I have built up personal resilience in the refuge of that love. This personal resilience was fostered and nurtured by the collective resilience I have experienced from the company of women in my life.

Most of the growth I have experienced and continue to experience in my life has not been from the achievement of the "summits," those big grand wins that mark milestones in our lives. While I am happy and privileged to have achieved those successes, the real story has been found in the time and the space that it took to get to the "peaks." It is the unhurried lengthening of those already overscheduled days, and the living of those days to the fullest, even when the air is cold and thin. The real achievement is in the safety and refuge gained in the formation of those true, loving relationships. It is revealed in the middle of the struggle, when we stay together and walk together, when the pace slows down to the level of discomfort that seems to make time stand still. It is the growth over 14,000 feet.

"Pole, pole."

Kristi McGuire is the founder of High Heel Brewing, an innovative craft beer company which introduced a line of craft beers designed to push the boundaries of traditional craft beer—developed by women, with women in mind. The company, which produces its beers in partnership with St. Louis-based Brew Hub, launched its first two brands, Slingback, an American Fruit Ale, and Too Hop'd to Handle, an Imperial IPA, in June of 2016. Slingback won two distinguished first-place gold medals, the first at the Great American Beer Festival in 2016 and the second at the Best of Craft Beer Festival in 2017. High Heel Brewing is planning to bring production and distribution to the St. Louis area in the first quarter of 2018.

Kristi, a beer lover and master brewer, brings more than 20 years of experience in brewing and product innovation. She has brewed, managed and created new brands from the ground up at breweries in Alaska, Texas, Georgia, California, Colorado, Missouri, New Hampshire and Florida during her time with Alaskan Brewing Company and Anheuser-Busch.

Continued

Kristi is a mother of four who lives life abundantly in St. Louis with her husband, Brian. She is a perpetual student and has studied at The University of Texas at El Paso, Texas A&M University, North Dakota State University, Kennesaw State, Georgia State, The University of California at Davis, Garrett Theological Seminary and Eden Theological Seminary

Kristi is passionate about her ministry work and published her first children's book, *We Loved Anyway*, through her company The Good Prophet LLC. Kristi loves to travel and spend time with her family, especially if it involves a stop at a local brewery to meet new friends over a really great beer.

Kristi McGuire
High Heel Brewing
highheelbrewing.com

Facebook: facebook.com/highheelbeer
Twitter: twitter.com/highheelbeer
Instagram: instagram.com/highheelbeer

The Good Prophet
goodprophet.com

Facebook: facebook.com/GoodProphetLLC
Twitter: twitter.com/thegoodprophet
Instagram: instagram.com/thegoodprophet

Change Your Heart

On July 10, 2017, I was unceremoniously walked out of my fifth and final corporate job. The conversation went something like this, "You're doing a great job, and we're just going in a different direction. It's a purely financial decision."

I was sent to my desk to pick up my belongings and leave. Fortunately, I had learned from experience that a clean desk policy is the best; I was able to stuff my few pieces of personal flair into my bag and walk out with my head high and my dignity intact.

It hadn't always been that way for me.

Wisdom is something we acquire as we gain experience. I don't want to say "get old," but you know what I mean. Remembering how I learned about true wisdom taught me how important it is to change your heart.

Flash back a few years to another time when I didn't handle a similar situation as well. Out of the blue one day, I got a call from the HR man where I was working at the time asking me to swing over to the factory where his office was located for a chat. Driving over, I was totally oblivious to the dramatic shift my life was about to take.

When I walked into the HR office and saw my current manager, Dick, sitting there, I realized this wasn't an ordinary meeting.

I was on high alert when the HR man said, "Dick, here, has been working on some organizational changes and you are no longer needed in the organization."

My first thought was that he was crazy—this couldn't be true. I was a director, the leader of a highly functioning team of eleven employees! They all loved me, didn't they? I had been working my ass off for five years to build this team and now I was no longer needed? How could this be happening?

Then it got interesting. The HR man proceeded to push a document across the table that was an account of all of the grievances Dick had against me. A list he had been keeping since becoming my new manager eight months earlier. As I read through the account of all my alleged crimes, I was shocked by the lack of truth and the level of detail involved. He had been keeping a secret diary!

The HR man seemed to think I had seen the document before, and when I told him I had no knowledge of the document nor conversations with Dick about any of these items, a look came over his face that told me he knew he had been duped. Dick had made a case against my performance without presenting any of the information to me or having any performance conversations. How could he have done this as most of the grievances were made up? Here we were, the three of us in the HR man's office, me sobbing and wailing (very classy, I know), the HR man confused, and Dick just sitting there with a smug look on his face.

I was devastated, to say the least. Everything I had worked for came crashing down around me at that moment, and my disdain—maybe even a little hatred—for this man was intense. How could this be happening? How could they be doing this to me? Where was the justice? Let's just say this was not my finest moment. I seriously could not get a grip in front of these two. I was humiliated to say the least.

Nonetheless, corporate policies and procedures prevailed. I wasn't fired from the company at that moment, but offered a demotion to a crappy job in government sales, a fate worse than death (or so I thought at the time). I was given the weekend to think it over and was ushered out the door. I was devastated as I realized I was no longer needed in a job that I loved.

Over the weekend, I decided I had to take the job because I needed the money as I had two kids getting ready to graduate from high school and start college. I went into my office that Sunday to gather my things. I had accumulated a lot of stuff over the years. Lesson learned: never have more in your office or cube than you can pack in one bag or box in order to walk out with your dignity intact.

On Monday morning, I reported to the government sales department. Everyone was confused. Why was Lynne Hayes, who had been a director on Friday, sitting in a cube (crying mostly, I'm embarrassed to admit) on Monday morning?

It was a disaster. The manager of the department didn't want me. I didn't want to be there. I had one sweet coworker who had coffee with me every day and listened to my "Woe is Me" story, but that got old for him pretty quickly.

I was willing to learn the job, but my heart wasn't in it. I was mad. I was humiliated. I was so ashamed. The shame I felt was strong. I couldn't believe I hadn't been more aware of the jeopardy I was in with Dick. He had been building a case against me and I was completely unaware.

I felt like I had let everyone down. My old team called me one at a time, but didn't really want to talk—I was damaged goods. One of my former employees came over to see me at my new job and brought me a coffee mug. It felt like a visit in the nursing home and I was the elderly patient. My self-esteem was zero and I was a disaster.

This all happened as I was attending a leadership development class Dick had approved. One week during this class I was a high-achieving director, and the next I was a sniveling wreck of a government sales rep. That class and that coach were monumental in my life. A change of heart was needed!

After my demotion, the HR man checked in with me on occasion to see how I was doing. I cried every time I talked to him. I told him I needed a coach, a third party non-judgmental observer. (looking back, I probably needed a counselor, but I got through it). I asked if I could have Pam, the leadership training facilitator, as a coach (I already had a relationship with her). He agreed. This was the start of my turnaround.

At the depth of my despair, for the first time in my professional life, Pam helped me see the only thing I could really control was me: my feelings, my words, my reactions. This was difficult for a self-described, sociopathic control freak like me.

Pam gently coached me to understand that I had to fix me; Dick had moved on. I was using all of my energy to hate him and be mad at the situation. I'll never forget her saying, "Do you think he has spent one minute thinking about you?" Of course not. This is an amazing lesson that I have kept with me and helped others realize when they feel that someone has "done them wrong." You control you.

The real lesson: I had to change my heart. Not just my thoughts, but how I felt in my heart. I was so devastated and angry over what he had done to me that I was in a bad place. I had to forgive him.

And here's the deal: to forgive him in my mind wasn't enough for me. I wanted to sit down across the table and forgive him out loud. Even if he didn't need it, I did. I arranged a meeting with the HR man, Dick, and myself. HR-man and Dick on one side of the table, me on the other. Here are the words I said:

"What happened, happened. It can't be changed. I think it was unfair. You know the truth and I know the truth. I have had some really bad days. But here's what I know for sure. You are human and I am human, and I'm the only one that can change me. I want you to know that I still don't agree with your decision or the way it went down. But I forgive you. Even if you don't need me to, I do."

And that was it. It was done. From that day, I learned that changing my heart was more important than changing my mind. I have practiced it relentlessly and fail at it often. It's more than empathy or giving people the benefit of the doubt. It's about digging deep and knowing only you can control you. It's one of life's most precious lessons.

What I've learned is that humans are messy. We have to be whole-hearted about ourselves if we want to change. The boss always wins. Once a decision has been made, you need to figure out how to reorganize. At the end of the day, it's a job. You get to choose. I chose to change my heart, rise above, and go out on my own. I'm looking forward to all of the possibilities.

Lynne Hayes is the founder of Edgehill Consultants, a new consultancy. Our motto is "Let's work on work."

Lynne has been an instructional designer, teacher and motivator for over 20 years. Her preferred title, Learning Leader, is only the beginning of her diverse resume. From leading national sales programs, increasing organizational collaboration, formulating better corporate communication styles and leading executive leadership sessions, Lynne has developed efficient and effective programs which last.

One of the first questions she'll ask is, "How can I help?" With a strong understanding of the changing workforce, she is an innovator when it comes to adapting traditional leadership styles with the unique challenges facing our modern workplace.

Lynne customizes leadership coaching, sales training, and communication workshops to fit every audience, from startup to Fortune 500 Company. Her professional interests include: generations in the workplace, sales team motivation and leadership

Continued

development. With her dynamic mix of encouragement, tools, passion and facts, she helps people add value to what they do every day.

When she is not traveling outside of St. Louis, Lynne loves to spend time playing ball with her rescue pup Mabel, early morning runs and cycling classes, coffee with her husband John, and contributing motherly words of wisdom to group texts with her grown-up kids, Emmy and Sam and Sam's wife, Samantha.

Lynne Hayes
lynne.hayes@edgehill.co
edgehill.co

Linkedin: linkedin.com/in/lynne-hayes-0331b66/

This Baby Won't Change a Thing

Much like, "I'll be able to wear this bridesmaid's dress again," or "I'll go to the gym after work today," telling myself that having a baby, "Won't change a thing," wasn't exactly accurate. At age 28, I liked my life exactly as it was. I had my dream job at Washington University, I owned an adventure education business on the side, I was in love with my rocket-scientist boyfriend, and I lived blissfully alone in a pristine apartment. So, when I found out I was pregnant in December 1994, I reassured myself: "This baby won't change a thing."

I did what every Type A career woman would do—I planned. My baby, who I had since learned was a boy, was due just before the biggest week of my year: freshman orientation. I scheduled a C-section for two weeks before my due date, figuring I'd have plenty of time to recover, get to know my baby, and be back in my heels and nylons in time for work.

I began to have second thoughts after my doctor gave me a book called *"What to Expect When You're Expecting"* by Heidi Murkof and Sharon Mazel. I read ahead to the section on recovering from Cesarean birth. I finally understood this was major abdominal surgery. I'd never had surgery before. I also learned that a vaginal birth is better for the baby, better for the mother, and allows the partner to be more involved. So I changed course.

I signed up for a twelve-week class in natural childbirth. I quickly became all but obsessed with having a natural birth.

I went into labor just days before my due date. With the help of my coach, I spent the majority of labor at home, arriving at the hospital in time to push. At one point during contractions, I broke down and asked for pain medication. Our nurse, knowing our goal of a natural birth, asked me to focus on what I was feeling and describe it to her. After thinking I said, "It's just really intense pressure."

She replied, "We don't have medicine for pressure," a wink in her voice.

At 12:36 A.M. on August 9, our baby boy entered the world. As he came out, he looked right into his father's eyes. Our doctor handed him to us. We were in love, in awe, overjoyed. At that moment, I realized what people meant when they talked about unconditional love.

I was overflowing with energy and adrenaline in the wake of my natural birth. The nurses warned me, encouraging me to take pain medication.

"I just had a natural childbirth," I thought. "I'll be fine."

I woke up to a crying baby feeling like a Mack Truck had hit me. This physical pain marked the beginning of a battle with depression and anxiety I had never expected or learned how to deal with. I had been so prepared for birth, but I was so unprepared for what came after.

Just twenty hours later, we sat in our living room staring at each other in silence as our baby slept. We had no idea what to do. I remember saying things during my pregnancy like, "I babysat for lots of kids! Caring for a baby is easy." I had never felt so unsure and overwhelmed.

During my maternity leave, I planned to work on several projects. Instead, I spent twelve weeks in a depressed and overwhelmed fog, barely finding time to shower. The phrase "sleeping like a baby" should be stricken from our language. My baby did not sleep for more than two hours at a time, and even then, he wanted to sleep on me. I went back to work fraught with anxiety about leaving my baby. Within months of returning to work, I gave notice.

Despite all of the joy this baby had brought into my life, I felt an almost unbearable weight of depression on my shoulders, even into his first year. I talked repeatedly to my doctor about it, but I was told that I would get better on my own, in time. That just didn't happen.

I finally got help for my postpartum depression and anxiety when my son was eighteen months old. Another young mom who was having similar struggles moved in next door to me. She saved my life; together we went out and found a community of moms. It was in these peer support groups that I began to heal. I realized I didn't need to suffer for as long as I did. I could've gotten help if I'd talked to someone who understood. I thought I could do it all on my own, but it became clear to me that it takes a village.

I decided then, I wanted to be part of the village that prepares other moms and their partners not just for birth, but also for what happens after. It seemed the best way to do this was through becoming a childbirth educator.

After taking the most comprehensive natural childbirth certification course I could find, I obtained my certification in August 1998. In December, I taught my first class and attended my first birth as a doula I felt completely in awe standing in the presence of miracles, watching couples prepare and bring their babies into the world. People talk about pregnancy and birth being hard, but what I really saw was that women are powerful.

I began to build my birth business village just as I had built my mommy village. I reached out to women in business that I looked up to and enlisted their input, creating my own personal Board of Trustees. These amazing women gave of their time and energy to help me create a birth business and describe it in words I hadn't been able to come up with on my own. In 2003, the term Newborn Family Coach was born. The tagline "Delivering Calm & Confident Parents to Newborn Babies" rolled out just like the placenta follows the baby.

My vision of empowering expectant families from pre-conception through the birthing years was blossoming, as I became the first childbirth educator in the St. Louis area to offer birth and postpartum doula services. As the Newborn Family Coach, I gave expectant parents the opportunity to receive continuous support from conception through that first joyful and challenging year.

It became evident that empowering families through my own individual work was not enough. The village that surrounded these parents needed an overhaul. In those early days, it was typical for childbirth educators to operate from a scarcity mindset. Birth doulas were a new concept for couples, hospitals, doctors, and nurses. There was an "Us vs. Them" mentality between doulas and other birth professionals, which was not helping anyone. After working for Barnes Hospital as a staff doula, I saw how childbirth educators and doulas played a significant role in bringing humanity into childbirth.

I knew in my heart that creating positive relationships with nurses, doctors, prenatal yoga instructors, massage therapists, midwives, family-supportive local businesses, and other childbirth educators was the key to improving birth options for all expectant parents. I was also very aware that there were more than enough clients for all of us. My conversations with other childbirth educators of various methods led to the creation of The Alliance of Childbirth Educators (ACE-STL). Working together, we put an end to that scarcity mindset and forged bonds that serve all expectant parents. We met monthly, hosted talks with obstetricians sponsored the St. Louis Improving Birth Rally, and raised the level of collaboration among birth professionals that continues today.

After working closely with those amazing women of ACE-STL, I knew I wanted to turn my solo practice into a partnership. I reached out to a few of the most progressive and experienced birth professionals in the St. Louis area. Together, we created what is now called Spectrum Birth Services. Our vision includes elevating the childbirth education and birth doula professions in the eyes of expectant parents and those who serve them.

Nearly twenty years have passed since I taught my first childbirth class and attended my first birth as a doula. The birth world has changed significantly, even opening up to embrace the idea that a mother's mental health is as important as her uterus. I'm truly grateful for the local businesses and services created by moms for moms like Mother-to-Mother, Kangaroo Kids, and the Family Center. I am proud to carry on the tradition of serving other moms in the greater St. Louis area in both my business, Spectrum Birth Services, and as the Postpartum Resource Coordinator for the MOMS Line. Expectant and postpartum moms can choose from many different types of educational and support options including maternal mental health professional and peer support. Moms can even get help for perinatal depression and anxiety by calling this one number, The MOMS Line, 314-768-MOMS.

My vision for the future includes a world where the mind, body, and spirit of pregnant and postpartum women are treated as equally important. At Spectrum Birth Services, we know expectant and newborn families are whole and dynamic beings on a miraculous journey.

It turned out that I was wrong all those years ago: having a baby changed everything. And I wouldn't have it any other way.

Kim Martino-Sexton, The Newborn Family Coach, has spent the past twenty years creating a career in the birth world after her first natural childbirth changed her life. She went from a high-powered career woman who was never going to have children to making her own baby food and teaching natural childbirth classes.

Today, Kim is the Co-Owner of Spectrum Birth Services LLC and the Postpartum Resource Coordinator for SSM St. Mary's Hospital responsible for The MOMS Line. She delights in delivering calm and confident parents to newborn babies through preconception coaching, childbirth education classes, birth and postpartum doula services, and perinatal mood and anxiety peer coaching. She has helped hundreds couples have their best birth and newborn family years.

At home, she is known as the "Mominator," an endearing term bestowed upon her by her rocket scientist husband and two amazing sons. She loves Sunday family dinners, walking her golden doodle Sadie, singing, reading science fiction romance novels, and being her own boss.

Continued

Kim Martino-Sexton
314-265-7407
Kim1@spectrumbirth.com
SpectrumBirth.com
ssmhealth.com/maternity/moms-line-stl

Facebook: facebook.com/SpectrumBirth/
Pinterest: pinterest.com/spectrumbirth/
Instagram: instagram.com/spectrumbirth/

Women and Wealth

What I Learned About the Workforce & What it Means to be a Woman

My first real job out of college was with a large national broker dealer. I can still remember my first interview—seeing all those fancy cars in the parking lot and brokers in their expensive suits, high-fiving each other across their desks. Right then, I knew this was the place for me. I wanted to be a broker, making money and having fun along with the rest of them. I was offered a position as a broker assistant and I took it, feeling confident I would work my way toward becoming a broker.

After working there for a few weeks, I started to see things I had initially missed. While nearly all the brokers were men, all the administrative and operational jobs were held by women. They were smart women, with extensive work and life experience, who could have held any number of professional positions.

I continued with my plan to become a broker—after all, there was absolutely no reason a woman couldn't hold that role. I inquired about joining the broker training program, only to be told I did not qualify. I did not have a "natural market" for prospects. However, I took note as one male college graduate was hired after the next, and placed directly into the broker training program. I was no different than they were; why couldn't I join the program?

I was raised to believe I was equal to men, and accomplishments didn't depend on gender, but hard work. My parents instilled in me the belief that I could do anything I chose, and a "man's job" should be no different than a woman's. I felt I had always been treated equally from elementary school through college graduation. Yet there I was, twenty-three years old, realizing the work world was different. I was somehow now considered to be less than my male colleagues.

I still remember how shocking this was. I felt as if I had been living in an egg my entire life—warm, cozy, and protected. Now, my egg had cracked, completely shattered onto the ground at my feet. All I wanted to do was reassemble my shell, piece it back together, and crawl back inside to escape from this strange new world where I did not like my pecking order.

After multiple failed attempts to join the training program, I found it difficult to come to work. I was embarrassed to be answering phones and doing menial tasks. I felt as though I was wasting my degree and my potential typing letters, while my male counterparts were launching their careers through an intensive multimonth training program. Even though I knew I was capable of more, I was beginning to doubt myself.

I looked around at the other women working alongside me. No one was talking about what they learned or what they might do next. Were they happy there? How many of them felt just like I did, but decided it was easier to consign themselves to the job at hand?

The men and women in the office seemed to be divided by an invisible fence, with plenty of gender-bashing on either side. Recognizing this, I no longer felt shame about my role. I felt anger—hot anger—and lots of it.

I began to think about finding a new job. I spoke with another brokerage firm, but once again heard that I had "no natural market." After a tour of the office and an introduction to some of the youngest, all male associates, I was beginning to wonder about investments as a career. Could there be more here I wasn't thinking of?

Not ready to settle, I continued my search. I began looking into opportunities at accounting firms, with departments that offered not only income tax planning, but investments, cash flow modeling, and estate planning as well. I was intrigued. I immediately sent resumes to a couple of these big five firms. After multiple rounds of interviews, I received two offers. I chose the one with a female partner who espoused education, and I never looked back.

My first day was a welcome surprise. I was given all the resources I would need for success, including a full training calendar. As I headed toward my car to go home, I felt good. Different. Taller, even. (If you've ever seen me in flats, you'll know this was significant!)

Right away, I noticed the associates, managers, directors, and partners were both female and male, across a staff of hundreds of employees. What a refreshing change! Did I say I wanted training? I got my wish and then some. I was sent to conferences, took dozens of online courses, read industry materials, and began studying for the Certified Financial Planner (CFP®) program.

Not only did this place look different, it was different. Everyone was expected to learn and work hard, and when you did, you were recognized. I was in the right place, part of a growing team. Having opportunity, support and resources—and being held accountable for my work—makes all the difference in the world.

Not only was I happy to be out of my shell, I was proud of myself for breaking through. I wondered, "Could I help other women do the same?"

This experience shaped my path forward. Let's face it—the financial services industry has ignored women for decades. Not just women advisors, but more importantly, women investors.

As I continued my career, I began to realize that what I experienced as a young woman entering finance is similar to what women investors face. While women are smart and capable, the industry was designed to cater to their husbands, brothers, and fathers. Historically, what women brought to the table was not valued. And for many women, their experience in working with a financial advisor left them questioning their ability.

The financial services industry also isn't easily adaptable to the realities of being a woman. We're at a disadvantage from the start—earning fewer dollars than men, often due to breaks in the workforce, as well as the very real gender gap (which is shrinking but still exists). We also tend to live longer than men, prompting those questions, "Will I have enough for retirement? How do I ensure I have extra to help support aging parents and children? Will I be okay?"

This uncertainty can take the wind right out of our sails. Working in this industry, I started to see women disengage and delegate financial management. Not only the day-to-day decisions, but the big strategic ones as well. This is when I realized it was time to swing the pendulum in the other direction. It was time to create a gender-balanced business—one that helps women build financial competency and, ultimately, confidence. One that gives women a place where their voices are heard, their opinions matter, and their unique life experiences are considered. A place where their desires and fears are placed center stage.

It all begins with the end in mind.

We all need permission to dream—to imagine what is possible in our futures. How do we want to support our communities or families? Only after we have defined our purpose, filled with significance and meaning, can we begin to figure out how money fits into this vision. Now, we are making important progress. Guess what comes next? Empowerment. Freedom. Time to unwind, reengage, and exit the work hamster wheel.

As a woman who had to build my competency and rebuild my confidence, I wanted to help other women do the same. That's why I adopted a gender lens, to build a wealth management practice for women and the men who love them. One that helps each of us understand the big picture, our motivations and our hopes and fears, and the lasting effects of our financial decisions.

I am thankful for my parents for raising me with confidence and high efficacy, believing I am worthy of success. I am also appreciative of those early experiences, as they had a profound impact on my emotions and drive.

I have come full circle. I started in this industry as a woman who was ignored, along with my peers. Now, I have the courage to live my life, true to myself and not the life others expect of me. I help women own their own financial futures, full of purpose and contentment, ready for the life each of us wants to live.

If you educate, engage, and empower a woman, then you can sit back and watch her fly. Indeed, I am enjoying the packed flight.

> "She took a leap of faith and grew her wings on the way down."
>
> —David Brinkley

Shannon Moenkhaus is focused on helping individuals and families achieve their financial goals. Her firm, Clarity Financial Planners, is committed to providing evidence-based investing, total financial life management, and lifelong learning to empower others to have a brighter financial future. In particular, she is passionate about helping women embrace responsibility for their finances and reach their goals.

A lifelong Missourian, Shannon spent her summers with her grandparents, taking care of family and community. Her memories of delivering food and developing friendships with the residents in her family's nursing home set her values early: take care of those who put their trust in you.

Shannon has spoken on gender inequality in the workforce for the Women's Foundation of Greater St. Louis, RISE Collaborative Workspace and Women & Wealth for Washington University – Olin Business School. She has also taught financial literacy

Continued

and other classes for UMSL, Entrepreneurs Organization, Tiger 21, Enterprise University, BAM Alliance, and others.

She has worked with Junior Achievement, served on the board for Central Institute for the Deaf, and is actively involved with Presidents Council and Logos School.

Shannon enjoys spending time hiking, paddling and four-wheeling just outside her family's 150-year-old tiny house on the Black River.

Shannon Moenkhaus, CFP®
Clarity Financial Planners
shannon@Clarityfinancialplanners.com

YKNOT Me?

My Journey to Craft the Career of My Dreams

I t was the day I had worked hard for. The day that made my blood, sweat, tears, late nights, and early mornings worth it. It was the end of one chapter and the beginning of another. It was May 17, 2014, the day I graduated with a Bachelor of Science in Health Management with a minor in Theological Studies from Saint Louis University. It was a big "check" off of my life to-do list.

Graduation cap? Check. Graduation robe? Check. Bright smile? Check. Hope? Check. Excitement? Check. #BlackGirl-Magic? Check. The start of my dreams coming true? Check.

As I walked down the aisle to receive my degree—happy, unstoppable, and optimistic—I had no idea my dreams of life after college would be so different from my reality. I envisioned myself making a five-figure salary or more per year, and based on the way the school set it up, it was exactly what I should have expected.

However, I tried everything I could to secure a position related to my degree and interest—human resources—but most jobs wanted five or more years of experience. I hit dead end after dead end and immediately after graduation settled for a part-time paid position as an intern at a small workforce staffing company, making a few cents above minimum wage.

I was teased and frowned upon for making so little money with my fancy degree, thinking I was tricking the system, knowing one day I was going to be a top human resources executive. I was "gaining experience" while working toward my Master of Arts in Human Resources Management at Webster University. But the internship was terrible and downright unethical. More than learning what to do in human resources, I learned what not to do. I witnessed discriminatory hiring practices and learned why so many people find it difficult to advance in life.

My checklist for life changed quickly. Anxiety? Check. Depression? Check. Frustration? Check. The only "good" thing, I wasn't the only one experiencing these feelings. My friends were too. So, I wasn't alone, but I still didn't know what to do.

In October 2014, I left the internship to accept a position as a part-time office coordinator with a leading healthcare organization. My goal was to become vice president of human resources or chief human resources officer, but I quickly learned that it wasn't that easy. All the legalities and hush-hush steps about how you can move up the ladder told me that I was stuck, and I felt undervalued. I applied to 150 jobs and could not move anywhere, not even into a full-time job at the organization.

My life checklist changed again. Shame? Check. Embarrassment? Check. "Why?" you might ask. Well, there are these things called hopes, dreams, and expectations that other people have for you, and if you don't meet them, you feel like a failure. Yes, I spent all of this money to get a degree from SLU, and yes, I was an office coordinator. Even worse, my SLU peers' and my parents' friends made me feel like I'd wasted all my scholarships and tuition money.

Then, I remembered what Professor Kennedy at Webster used to say, "Sometimes you have to leave a company for them to see your value."

In July 2015, I started a job as a compliance associate with a healthcare staffing firm. Yeah, it sounds fancy—I had business cards, my own office, and everything looked great. The pay was mediocre, but no one else knew it. I had finally "made it," or at least that's what people thought. Soon, I learned the company cared more about sales than people. Their mentality was quantity over quality. I also saw that I couldn't advance. Even more, the culture was toxic. My coworkers and managers talked about me behind my back because I wouldn't engage in corporate politics. I was left out of company lunches. The office I used to brag about turned into the office I hid in and never left. Every day of my last three months at this company, I cried.

In July 2016, I returned to the leading healthcare organization where I was an office coordinator, and this time I was an administrator. Based on the job title alone, I was sure that I'd be running things. I was like, "Momma I made it! I'm a hospital administrator." My parents passed my business cards out like they were Halloween candy. For me, it was a dream-come-true. Not only was I able to combine all of my educational experiences, I had taken a step forward careerwise.

Then, all of my checklists from the past two years hit me at once. I soon found out my new position was three jobs in one. I was editing documents, folding brochures, and completing other administrative tasks that had nothing to do with my degree. I was treated like and called a secretary, office coordinator, and administrative assistant. Once again, I was stuck in corporate limbo, and wondered, "What's next?"

My life checklist was becoming pretty repetitive. Unhappy? Check. Meager pay? Check. Lack of opportunities for advancement? Check. Expectations that are far from reality? Check.

Instead of leaving one job to go to another, I enrolled in the Doctorate in Health Professions Education program at Logan University. I also decided to focus on the company I launched in December 2015, YKNOT Consulting LLC—a human resources development firm for Generation Ys focused on career improvement.

Finally, my life checklist was renewed and infused with hope. Passion? Check. Purpose? Check. Helping others make their dreams come true? Check.

I started YKNOT because of how much I struggled to climb the corporate ladder, and felt like I wasn't good enough. I wanted to prevent as many people as I could from feeling the way my friends and I did. In college, you don't learn the hidden realities of corporate life, and it isn't right. Within my company, I help my peers with job and career coaching, especially those who have baby boomers as parents, because sometimes they just don't get us. From tailoring resumes to branding: using coursework to demonstrate skills, branding tips, confidence boosting, and interview preparation. I help clients with the entire job-seeking process.

YKNOT makes me feel like a superhero! I feel like I'm changing lives and bridging gaps. When I'm doing the work of

YKNOT, I feel like I'm finally living my purpose. It's not about the money or recognition, I see the sparks go off in people's eyes and I know I have found my calling. What I do now is help others with the response to the questions I've asked myself countless times: "Why can't I fulfill my potential? Why can't I do what I love? Why can't I build my dream instead of just helping someone else build theirs? Why can't I make my dreams come true? Why can't I start a business that transforms lives? Why can't I change the world? YKNOT me?!"

If it weren't for one failed job after another, I would not be where and who I am today. Trying to fit myself into boxes that weren't made for me got me here. Trying to put myself in boxes period, got me here. Every attempt at corporate "success" showed me the life I wanted had to be designed. With each disappointment, moment of frustration and anxious feeling, I learned more about myself. Each one of these experiences—in some way—prepared me for my dream to help other people achieve their dreams.

My journey has taught me to create for myself what is not readily available to me. If the job I dream of doesn't exist, or if I can't secure it through traditional employment, then I have the power, experience, and knowledge necessary to create it. I've also learned to do what values me, my skills, and my interests. My career is about more than receiving a paycheck, having a fancy title, or the illusion of success. My career is about doing what challenges my interests and skills, what forces me to grow.

I learned to choose myself over waiting for others to choose me by way of being offered a job. I see that sometimes you have to let go, so what you desire can come to you. I also see there is no such thing as what you're "supposed" to do, but what makes you happy. To pursue your dreams and build a life you love, you must connect with your inner being, follow your intuition, and choose what moves you. So, anytime you wonder whether you're enough, or the right person, personality, or skin color, if you have the right background or experience, when you doubt your talents or potential, ask yourself this question: YKNOT me? Then respond by doing what you need to do to make it happen.

Maurya Dominica Cockrell is an empire builder and mogul maker. As Founder and CEO, she officially launched YKNOT Consulting LLC in 2015. YKNOT Consulting LLC is a St. Louis-based human resources development company that helps Millennials navigate and develop their careers and/or small businesses; assists corporations with employee engagement; and promotes inter-generational collaboration.

A strategic, visionary thinker, Maurya is passionate about inspiring Gen Y to cultivate a growth mindset in order to optimize their full potential. Through workshops, individual consultations, presentations and boot camps, Maurya shares her expertise in the areas of interpersonal effectiveness, communication skills, personal strategic planning, and self-care. Her clients include private schools, universities, law firms, construction companies, fast food chains, and other local businesses.

In addition to operating YKNOT Consulting LLC, Maurya owns and operates multiple other business ventures. In her spare time, she enjoys reading, performing with her dad's smooth jazz

Continued

band, serving on young professionals boards, and volunteering as a member of Delta Sigma Theta Sorority, Incorporated.

Maurya holds a Bachelor of Science in Health Management from Saint Louis University with a minor in Theology, and a Master of Arts from Webster University in Human Resources Management. She is currently pursuing a Doctorate in Health Professions Education from Logan University.

Maurya Dominica Cockrell
314-304-2051
consultyknot@gmail.com
ConsultYKNOT.com

Facebook: facebook.com/ConsultYKNOT
Twitter: twitter.com/YKNOTConsulting
Instagram: instagram.com/YKNOTConsultingLLC

The Reluctant Entrepreneur

"**I** will NEVER be like you! I will have a normal job at a big company where I get a dependable pay check!"

"We'll see," my dad smiled and looked up at me over his half-glasses, case files in his lap as he prepared for night court.

I stomped up the stairs.

Growing up in a home which seemed anything but stable made me crave security. I rejected a music scholarship, choosing to major in business with an emphasis in accounting, knowing I would always have a job that paid a living wage or better.

How did I end up starting my own CPA firm, which became-Farmer & Farley, LLC, going through the very struggles I dreaded and hoped to avoid? Although I had a deep desire to find a secure, dependable job, I was drawn to small businesses and their owners I served. Entrepreneurs fascinated me. Their vision and courage collided with my passion to help people. I caught the business ownership bug, even though for many years, I didn't recognize the similarities I shared with my clients.

Webster's defines an entrepreneur as "a person who organizes and manages an enterprise, especially a business, usually with considerable initiative and risk." My clients are willing to start and manage their own businesses, despite the risk. They don't allow fear to paralyze them. And they inspire me!

I suppose there are many roads to becoming a certified public accountant. And since I have been at this for thirty years, I imagine those roads have changed. When I started, my job as a staff accountant demanded long hours. At the end of a job we received review points, a list of questions, and errors to be corrected. I was undone by the process—absolutely dismantled! I was motivated by success and encouraged by accolades, but to say the criticism hurt doesn't begin to describe my experience.

I have since learned I was suffering from a fixed mindset. I thought I needed to know everything in order to be successful. In fact, I was learning and growing like crazy through this process. The hardness of the fixed mindset—that mistakes were paralyzing and the shame was insurmountable—softened as I confronted mistakes, overcame, and learned from them. Eventually, I learned to recognize I am human and will make mistakes. I began to embrace each mistake as an opportunity to learn and grow.

It wasn't just the sting of facing my imperfection and learning how to grow from criticism. I was a frustrated leader. In my new profession, as part of a firm, I didn't see a path to leadership. My favorite parts of high school involved leadership. We were told over and over we would be leaders as adults. As a leader in high school—president of my senior class and a captain on the cheerleading squad—I loved organizing events and being involved in decision-making. But the position of being a staff accountant, and even that of a supervisor, didn't offer leadership opportunities.

There was no teamwork involved in working alone the vast majority of the time.

My first child was born as I traversed this rough road. I was surprised by my desire to care for her. When combined with the emotional challenges of my career, I was ambivalent in charting my professional future. My mentor had returned to school after her children were in high school and changed professions. She worked part-time year-round, and inspired me to balance family and profession by not being too caught up in the grind.

In order to be licensed as a certified public accountant, in addition to passing the CPA exam, I was required to fulfill a minimum of two years of public accounting work experience. Many people leave public accounting once this requirement is met.

So after fulfilling my two years, I began interviewing with large corporations for a variety of available positions. Yet as I considered each opening, I feared the boredom of monotony detailed in the job descriptions. Ultimately, I declined every offer.

Having gained the valuable skills of working in a small firm performing a wide variety of assignments, it was easy for me to find a job as an employee in a small firm. This provided flexibility as I continued to grow my family and make a living. Although I didn't see the end I desired, I stuck with it.

I managed to work full-time during tax seasons and part-time the remainder of the year until my fifth child was nine months old. By this time, I realized if I wanted to gain the knowledge and skills to move to partner level, I would need to devote more time to my profession. My husband supported this decision and I began working long hours as a manager with a small local CPA firm as my husband cared for our children full-time for a few years.

I had our sixth child while working in a small firm undergoing rapid growth. It was so exciting to help clients create their businesses and watch them realize their dreams. I enjoyed forming relationships and building trust, learning so much along the way. I knew I would be a minority partner, but I was thrilled to be part of a team.

Investing more hours increased my competency dramatically. Additionally, I was able to exercise leadership and build a team. But even so, something was missing. Envisioning myself as a minority partner in this small firm was losing its luster.

I interviewed at a large local firm and was offered a position. But the position offered a sliver of my current job responsibilities. Again, I feared boredom and couldn't accept the position. This closed an avenue of growth professionally for me, but I simply wasn't willing to narrow my focus which would have been required to accept a position at a larger firm. At the same time, I couldn't envision myself as a minority partner in the small firm where I was working.

I was at a crossroads.

I was terrified to go out on my own, but my extended family gave me a big project that I could use to jumpstart my business. I became the trustee for a family member's estate, a project I was able to bill as the first client of Elizabeth L. Farmer CPA, LLC. With the encouragement of friends, I did it—I started my own firm and embarked on the journey of a lifetime!

Ironically, my journey began much like my father's. I was in an office of attorneys sharing overhead. I was the only CPA hoping to grow a business, sharing space, and a receptionist, but the business was mine to grow. I think I expected a smooth journey. Sure, I expected to have to work hard, but I was in the driver's seat with no one to please but my clients. I knew I could work hard—that was the easy part. The hard part was realizing how much I needed to learn to run my own business.

Where to begin to describe the learning that ensued? In some ways everything before that point was academic. Now, I was in the fire with my clients. I understood the panic of upcoming payroll. Other people and their families were dependent upon my getting this right.

It was easy to get new clients to let me help them— getting paid was the challenge. Yet I understood their predicament. Around every corner was a new barrier, another unforeseen delay in a secure, predictable business. The temptation to quit, merge— do ANYTHING to find the security I craved—intensified with every point of adversity.

Many of the obstacles I faced were self-erected walls. It seemed like I must have been building them in my sleep. I was unaware of how my decisions or delayed decisions were impacting the trajectory of my business. I encouraged my clients to set goals and confront obstacles. Was I willing to offer myself the same advice?

Yes.

I began setting goals and creating accountability by sharing the goals with my team. When obstacles slowed progress, I made myself my client. In fact, the goals for my business were given proper priority and voila, walls came down. I was no longer the girl looking for someone else to provide the elusive security I had desired.

I have become like my clients who succeed—determined to survive and thrive. I am willing to do the difficult inner work essential to open the road to success for the company I am building with my team.

I may have started reluctantly, but no longer. I am a woman on the rise! I am an eager, optimistic, risk-taker with the confidence to live my dream.

Elizabeth L. Farmer is a mother of six children, a certified public accountant, and the founder of Farmer & Farley. She serves as a trusted advisor for individuals and small business owners, helping them improve their tax position.

Elizabeth works hard to balance time and focus between her various roles. The challenge of finding equilibrium contributed to her starting a firm of her own, one which aims to help others find their balance. Taking her own advice, she adopted a cloud-based working environment at Farmer & Farley, providing flexibility for both employees and clients.

Elizabeth is a member of the American Institute of Certified Public Accountants and Missouri Society of Certified Public Accountants.

Continued

Elizabeth Farmer
efarmer@farmerfarleycpa.com
farmer-cpa.com

Facebook: facebook.com/efarmercpa
Linkedin: linkedin.com/company/farmer-&-farley-llc/
Yelp: yelp.com/biz/farmer-and-farley-cpa-creve-coeur

Listening to
the Messages

L ife is a journey in which we can make choices to contribute to others in a positive way. Having a mindset of being a life-long learner and being adaptable to change will make you a stronger individual and more adept in dealing with life's ebbs and flows. The one key philosophy that has served me most in this life is trusting the interconnectedness of the world. For me, this means being open to the messages all around, whether they come from deep inside, from those who love you unconditionally, or from those who have passed who are still pushing you forward.

In many ways, I know my dad is my guardian angel. It is not easy to explain, but it is a deep feeling of familiarity, connected-ness, and understanding. The feeling of support, which began at birth, has continued beyond his death. I remember the long walks we would take discussing life and business. He seemed to have intuitiveness about him. He also had a huge heart, making those he connected with feel they were his only priority. I trusted his advice, and though I didn't always take it, I knew it was coming from a place of support and wisdom. He was my teacher, and as the proverb says, "When the student is ready, the teacher will appear."

My dad told me many times he felt he had a guardian angel after his dad died when he was only thirteen. I feel fortunate I was with my dad when he died at the Tampa airport, and I feel his spirit is with me as strong as it was when he was here.

I was thirty-one when he died. Remembering that day at the airport, tears come to my eyes when I think about how I was by his side, talking to him, getting the paramedics, watching him die, finding my mom, calling my brothers, and then shockingly realizing I didn't know where my three kids were. My oldest was only five, my daughter three, and my youngest was six months and in a car seat. I panicked. Miraculously, someone appeared and told me it was all right and my kids were safe. I walked with a young man and saw my three children sitting on the floor in a circle. I had no idea how he got them or where he came from, but he helped me take them to the car and I thought as I left, he must have been an angel.

My dad died at the airport, but we followed the ambulance to the hospital anyway. That night at the hotel, I could feel his warmth around me. For many weeks, we communicated by lights turning off or on based on questions I asked him. Since then, my dad has come to me in my dreams, through specific signs and a medium.

The most impactful messages have come through two epiphanies. These epiphanies set my course in life. One kept me married to my husband who was an alcoholic. Our three children were all under the age of eight. We had been through extensive counseling, and I finally got him to commit to a couple's marriage repair weekend. I knew if we went, I would get the answer I needed. Either get divorced or repair our marriage. The therapy part was terrific and enlightening, but on our one night by ourselves we were back to our old selves. I went to bed that night knowing I had found my answer, we had to get divorced. I woke up early with overwhelming clarity. Do not divorce. Keep the family together and maintain control of your children's lives. It was amazingly clear and it felt right. Fast forward fourteen years, the silver lining is he became sober after more than a decade and now we are working on healing.

The second epiphany came to me this year. When my dad died of melanoma, he believed it was caused by him going to work putting stickers on cars at a local tourist attraction, getting burned to a crisp every day. This job led my dad to meet someone who owned gas stations. As soon as my dad turned sixteen, he went to work for him. That one decision led my dad on his path, which led him to a place beyond his furthest expectations, and gave him the platform to fulfill his life's purpose.

Even though he believes his constant exposure to the sun when he was young caused this progressive cancer, he might not have lived a life beyond expectations if his dad had not died tragically at a young age. All things happen for a reason. We are just not always clear on what that reason is. However, if we saddle up even when we are scared, and chose to move forward because we have made a conscious choice, we will find our purpose. It wasn't until now that we understood the decision he made would lead to my second epiphany.

This came when I had been CEO for five months. When the message came, it was with the same clarity of the first epiphany. For twenty-four years, I loved working in our family business with an overarching purpose of moving our family and company forward. I loved the people and working in retail operations, as well as the support departments that created the systems for individuals to become stronger in their personal and professional lives. While my dad was alive, he told many people that one day I would be running the company. No one could have predicted my Dad's early death, but through hard work, meritocracy, and perseverance, I did become CEO. It was a five-year transition plan that my brothers and I worked on with my mom, who took over the CEO role after my Dad passed. In that time, I earned my MBA, had a strong network, and a fabulous executive coach. Finding the coach is a story unto itself. It was a nationwide search, but I believe by being open to the messages around me and being a student who was ready, it led me to this teacher.

These messages led me to write a letter about my true purpose, which eventually led me to leaving my family business a few months later. I never could have predicted that leaving my family business would lead me to become the executive director of the very synagogue that my parents were married in, where my entire family had celebrated all life cycle events. I was moving from my family business to my spiritual family. It was a move that I feel deep inside was meant to be. This move came to me because I was open to listening to the messages around me.

In my new role, I have the platform to dedicate more time to repair the world. This phrase is a foundational principle in Reform Judaism: leave the world in a better way than we found it. This philosophy can apply to helping others, helping our environment, or taking the time to help others reach their full potential. Repairing the world takes courage, even when you feel scared.

I am a believer that the right people come into your life at the right time for a specific purpose. Someone in my network told me I had to meet Stacy Taubman. Little did I know that the coffee talk between Stacy and I would lead to a greater network at RISE Collaborative. As I sit here today, what we don't know is where this chapter in the RISE book will take me. I am certain I am on the right path. The medium I have visited three times since my dad passed confirmed my feeling that I am on the right path. Through the medium's messages and spiritual healing, I trust and know that I have a vast network of people behind me. Many are living and many have passed, but they are all pushing me forward.

Trust the messages and the interconnectedness. I encourage you to believe in yourself and listen to these messages around you. You are the only you there is! You have the ability to do so many great things in this life if you take care of your mind, body, spirit, and heart. With many blessings, may you always move forward, listen to the messages, and find your purpose.

Rachel Wallis Andreasson is the Executive Director of Congregation Temple Israel. Prior to joining Temple Israel, Rachel worked 24 years in various leadership positions at Wallis Companies, including being the first 2nd generation CEO. Wallis Companies is proud of their 1,100 team members throughout the state of Missouri and Southern Illinois who continue to carry on the legacy of Rachel's father, Bill Wallis.

Prior to joining Wallis Companies in November 1993, she was the Training Coordinator at South Seas Plantation on Captiva Island, outside of Ft. Myers, FL. In 1991, Rachel earned a Bachelor of Management degree from Tulane University in New Orleans. She earned an MBA with honors from Olin Business School at Washington University in St. Louis in 2012. She was the founding President of the Crawford County Foundation in 2001 and currently serves as Secretary. Rachel serves on the Board of Directors for Wallis Companies as well as the National Association of Convenience Stores and is a Director for the Peoples Bank of Cuba.

Continued

A highlight of her professional career was being installed as the first female President of the Missouri Petroleum Marketers Association and served on its Board for 15 years and was awarded a Distinguished Service Award.

Rachel and her husband have three grown children, with whom they continue on life's journey together.

Rachel Wallis Andreasson
Temple Israel's website: ti-stl.org

Facebook: facebook.com/rachel.andreasson
Linkedin: linkedin.com/in/rachel-wallis-andreasson-ba358111/

Seeking a SOLution

"*Wake up! It's the last day of the month, and I have a job to do.*" *When I sold liquor for a living, the last day of the month stressed me out. Would my team make goal? What if we didn't? At the same time, I was excited about finishing strong. An adrenaline rush kicked in, humor got us through the day, and teamwork kept us motivated. We made it happen! Then, exhaustion set in. I thought, "I need a detox—somewhere to go to calm down, rejuvenate, and breathe. Sauna take me away!*"

An exciting career in big business had been a dream since I was little, wanting to follow in my dad's footsteps. His long career with Procter & Gamble inspired me to create campaigns and promote brands I loved. I passionately absorbed the world of business—the good and the bad. I took pride in learning as many functions as possible, with a goal to be well-rounded and add value to people and corporations. As a result, I landed a series of dream jobs: public relations for a major sports team, sales promotion for prestigious publishing houses, account services and supply chain management for the biggest franchise in the world, and sales and marketing for a global luxury wine and spirits company. I valued and appreciated the freedom to choose and move forward when a new calling came.

Chicago was an amazing place to live for eighteen years—I was able to seek and find fun times, amazing business opportunities, connections, friendships, and the diverse culture of a big city I had craved my whole life. Moving to St. Louis in 2013 offered progressive career potential and, finally, the gift of living in the same city as my parents and close family. A new job and a new city were a welcome challenge. I say challenge, because it was a time in my life when my faith was being tested. Yet, I had great ambition and hope for a bright future.

The world of wine and spirits was dynamic, and I savored this demanding lifestyle choice. My priceless experiences, working with a different cast of characters every day, riding the waves of trends kept me invigorated for years. The sales director position I accepted in St. Louis promised the opportunity to be part of a newly formed division tasked with changing the male-dominated corporate culture that was swirling around liquor distribution in Missouri. I love change, and I was up for the job of leading a team to glory in unchartered territory!

While I enjoyed the friendships and fun of working with a new team, the cutthroat nature and pressure to perform at all costs took a toll on my mind and body. Within one year, I was diagnosed with cancer and was suffering from extreme burnout. The once glamourous industry started to become a blackhole for me. I used to sell beverages I loved, now shots were a priority. Fireball was a phenomenon. How could I push something I didn't use myself? Our vice president commented it was a deal with the devil. Needing out, I promised myself I would have a new position within a year. Continuing to work hard, I believed the right opportunity would present itself in due time. Leaving gracefully and with a plan was essential. Understanding my why was crucial.

What was my true calling? Feeling brave and proud of myself for conquering many fears and learning valuable lessons along the way, I was open and determined to find my purpose. I was scared to leave a good-paying job in an industry I thrived in, but I prayed and surrendered to what was next for me. My soul was craving something fresh, as well as a healing environment. In November 2014 my stress was at an all-time high with year-end goals, the holidays being non-stop in my industry and the Ferguson verdict impacting the city. One Friday night while relaxing in the gym sauna, wishing there was a social alternative to drinking (well maybe high-end tequila and green juice could be included), as well as a healthy place to connect, I had a clear vision. Sometimes my greatest clarity comes while in my darkest hours. It was an "aha" moment.

I could not get the dream of opening a sauna business out of my mind.

Come January 2015, I was ready to make this my best year yet! The first chance I got, I took a trip to California to visit my friend, Jayme. We originally met at a temazcal ceremony during a yoga retreat in Tulum, Mexico in 2008 and became fast friends. Jayme has a nourishing spirit, and she gets me. When I confided in her about my idea, the look on her face was joyful confusion. Julie, Jayme's friend, had just opened The Sauna Studio, and she had never heard of anyone doing that before. Me either. I only knew of Russian bathhouses, Korean spas, and a few high-end wellness resorts focused on quality sauna therapy.

After speaking to Julie and scheduling a trip to visit her in April, I was inspired to take the leap of faith and execute my idea. I created a mini–plan and strategically figured out my departure from the fascinating world of wine and spirits. I made a promise to myself that I intended to keep.

Mentally, I only had two more end-of-the months in me, so June would be my goodbye to the life that no longer served me. Still struggling to sleep due to adrenal fatigue, a stressful work-place, and fears of the financial future ahead of me, I happily counted down the days. Before I could fully enjoy a summer of self-exploration and inner-work, finishing strong in my current position was the task at hand. Float STL, Women's Weekend with Dianna Lucas, and working with Johana Probst, a natural-born healer and shaman with a multi-dimensional energetic approach to processing life on a soul level, helped me during this transition.

Taking all my heart and grit with me, I was ready to reca-librate and live life on my own terms. Utilizing my previously acquired skills and trusting my intuition, I delighted in creating my own brand and becoming a true entrepreneur. The whole pro-cess was my own healing, my own soul sweat. Both literally and figuratively, I let go while absorbing the goodness of the Sun (Sol).

Sol Sweat, an infrared sauna studio, was open for business in November 2015. Exactly one year after that moment of pure inspi-ration in the gym sauna, my vision had become a reality. Living the dream for me continued in the form of sharing my wellness journey and wisdom with others. My mission was to bridge the gap between working in survival mode with finding peace in the moments and answering to yourself.

My Facebook post was the first time I shared my story with others. It went like this...

ARE YOU READY TO RELAX?
SOL SWEAT NOW OPEN!

Dear Friends and Family,

I take great pleasure in announcing that my new business, Sol Sweat, is officially open. For years, after working in fast-paced environments, I would seek heat to relax every chance I had. From hot yoga, to vacations in the sun, to steam rooms or saunas at expensive gyms or spas—I was willing to pay anything for that feeling. My vision was to find a passive, easy-access option for myself and others to reap those same benefits at an affordable price.

This is how Sol Sweat was created—a comfortable space that was private yet accessible to sit in your own state-of-the-art infrared sauna to relax, rejuvenate, and feel radiant.

Infrared saunas are an effective tool for natural healing and prevention. Infrared light has the ability to penetrate human tissue, which in turn produces a host of anti-aging benefits for overall healthier living. The heat stimulates your cardiovascular, lymphatic, and immune systems. This produces a deep, therapeutic, perspiration, releasing toxins, burning calories, and relaxing your muscles.

If you are looking to feel better, mind, body, and spirit, Sol Sweat is for you.

From that day forward, I was dedicated to finding solutions and options for better health for myself and others. Even though I had always been curious about new ways to prevent aging and sustain my energy, healing was now my job and I was passionate about it!

Life as an entrepreneur continues to be exciting. Awareness of who I am and what my why is have never been more apparent. Every day I wake up, so thankful for all my life experiences and appreciate how it got me where I am today. What I do now will get me to tomorrow. Spreading love and good energy is my mission.

One Life, One Sol.

Stacy Sullivan is an entrepreneur, zen marketer, closet comedian, and an advocate for living life as an adventure. She has swum with sharks in Belize, lived down the street from Barack Obama in Chicago, and aspired to be Wonder Woman growing up.

Experience working with innovative brands, incorporating her own lifestyle, was the stepping stone to founding Sol Sweat infrared sauna studio in 2015. Additional career highlights include launching Oprah's Book Club as a Sales Promotions Coordinator, living in Toronto to source product for the first McCafe, and sharing the fascinating story of Veuve Clicquot LaGrande Dame at Donna Karan's Women Who Inspire dinner.

Currently, she is an avid networker and active member of the St. Louis Startup Ecosystem. A graduate of the CET Fueling Innovation Accelerator program, she continues to participate in ventures dedicated to economic growth and leadership.

Continued

Excited to share efficient ways to increase ones' energy and vitality, she is eager to learn and educate. Check out her website and follow her as she launches Sol Seeks, a marketing platform and data dissemination utility for everything wellness. Email her and she will respond with a warm smile and enthusiasm to connect.

Stacy Sullivan
314-609-0555
stacy.sullivan@solseeks.com
solsweat.com

Facebook: facebook.com/solsweat/
Linkedin: linkedin.com/in/stacysullivan/

The Wisdom
of Challenges

As I read somewhere, all heroic journeys involve struggle and the willingness to pursue our dreams and learn more about ourselves. I've come to believe that we are all heroes on our journey of life. To learn the new lessons life presents and become a better person, we need to overcome our own challenges, which will look different for each of us.

My challenges have taught me my life story is worth sharing, and it's important for me to talk about it now. People have suggested I write about my story when I retire, yet when I heard about the RISE project, I knew I couldn't wait—now was the time. I knew it would be challenging to share what I've learned and lived. And I also know what I have learned could help others pursue their dreams.

I was born and raised in a large city in Russia. Technically, I am from the opposite side of the world. The time difference between St. Louis and my home town is exactly twelve hours.

The sense of freedom and entrepreneurial spirit were always part of my personality. After I graduated university with an engineering degree, I worked only once for someone prior to starting my first business.

My first business was a wholesale mobile phone company. I was in the right place at the right time as my company was the first mobile phone company in our city. More importantly, I had the courage and desire to try something completely new and see it through. As a result, the company was ranked the number- one company in the Siberian region in 2004-2005.

My second business, a luxury boutique, was completely different. I owned the first store in our city selling premium Swiss watches such as Cartier, Hublot, Gerard-Perregaux, plus high-end branded fine jewelry, and elite giftware. It was a beautiful business.

I felt I was blessed. I enjoyed my work, which was incredibly interesting and exciting. I loved feeling that my business was my own creation, it became part of my heart, and I was able to travel! Both businesses gave me the opportunity to visit more than thirty countries, and it was a fantastic experience of exploring diverse cultures and viewpoints.

At some point, though, life brought me unexpected challenges. The downside of success and travel was that I became too idealistic and ignored reality and danger. I ignored the fact that I was one of the few female business-owner in my industry. I thought it would be enough to conduct my business in a fair way while working hard. Unfortunately, I found out the hard way I was too vulnerable on my own.

My jewelry business became too public. I was on four magazine covers and featured in countless other publications being interviewed about my Swiss watches and jewelry business. Unfortunately, combined with client attention, it also brought the attention of some powerful people in our city.

It was 2008 and I was getting ready to become a mother for the second time. Pregnancy was a blessing for me, but it also made me vulnerable. After a series of unfortunate events, I let the wrong person enter into my confidence and give away partial control of my business.

In 2011, I decided to fight and protect my business and idealistic idea that women in Russia could have freedom and spirit and be successful business owners. The pre-election race began and I chose to support an independent candidate, which was a dangerous step. Though I had connections with clients and vendors, owning this business was no longer safe for me or my family. I understood I needed to leave my country in order to live the life I intended.

The goal was clear—I was ready to start my life over from zero in a new country. I had family in the United States, so we would never be completely alone. America is the land of opportunity, and I was driven to take my strengths and experience to this new country and create a better life for all of us.

Despite my best laid plans, it was not the end of challenges for me.

I was a single mom and couldn't take a sufficient amount of money with me. I thought my English was strong, but it wasn't good enough for me to secure a valuable corporate job that would enable me to grow and pay my bills. I was overqualified for the positions I was applying for, yet didn't have American experience, so my impressive resume fell flat. The frustration and disappointment were almost too much for me to handle. Finding a job became my Mission: Impossible.

On the other hand—and perhaps more valuable to my life and future than a job—I was blessed to have my family's support and meet so many amazing people who become my friends and helped me feel welcome in this new country. I had their emotional support, which got me through the most difficult times. Then three years ago, I met my husband, who became my best friend and a father for my little daughter.

I began to find employment—even if I was overqualified—and every new job brought me knowledge and experience, and developed my language. My values shifted, as I realized money doesn't bring you happiness, but your optimistic attitude and ability to enjoy simple pleasures will.

One of my mentors taught me to write down my goals to help guide my way and hold myself accountable. As part of that process, I asked myself, "How can I use my talents in the most efficient way to contribute to society and people?" I decided I wanted to work in the financial industry. I was very good with math and finding solutions and, as you know, math doesn't have one language—numbers and symbols transcend all spoken languages! It was a perfect fit, and I set a goal to work in finance.

If you have talents and a burning desire to develop them—you will be successful, whether that success comes early or late. Not only in finance, but in everything, if you have your purpose and desire.

Once I had a clear goal, lightning struck again. I was in the right place at the right time and took a position with New York Life Insurance Company. My hiring manager believed in me and gave me a chance, and it was exactly what I needed.

I passed three difficult certifications and became not just an agent, but a financial services professional. There is nothing as satisfying to me as getting to help families and business owners improve their lives by providing financial security and creating generational wealth. I have found my purpose—vastly different from the jewelry and lifestyle business I started in—but it's where I needed to end up.

In three years, I plan to open my own business again, but with backing by one of the strongest financial institutions in the world. I am finally on the right path toward an even greater level of life satisfaction than when I owned my business in Russia. And I'm setting even more ambitious goals: in five years I want to be one of the five most influential women in the financial industry in St. Louis.

This is not the end of my story. While I'm still not where I want to be in my life, this is still only the beginning of my journey.

If you share your goals with people who are ready to support you and wish you the best in your life, your goals are more likely to come true. I believe in supporting your goals and I hope that you believe in supporting mine.

And so I am asking for your help: I need you to be my accountability partners. Help keep me accountable for reaching my goal and know that I am here to help support you in reaching your goals, too! Send me an email and tell me your goals. Together, just like we do at RISE Collaborative, we can encourage, support, and wish the best for one another. Because we all deserve every happiness on our heroic journey called life.

Prior moving to the United States, Olga Sityaeva successfully started and grew companies in Russia with multimillion-dollar revenue in both retail and wholesale operations. Her background demonstrates entrepreneurial business ownership acumen which helped her to become a seasoned professional in the sales and marketing arena. Her previous and current work experience, combined with her degree in Engineering, has helped her to learn quickly, adapt to new roles, responsibilities, tasks, technologies/software, and environments. Olga's strengths include experience in cultivating professional interpersonal relationships with key customers and corporate leaders towards the goal of attracting new customers, retention and converting competitor's clients, team leadership and developing brand and marketing strategies.

After moving to the United States six years ago, Olga settled in St. Louis and in June 2016 became an Agent licensed to sell insurance through New York Life Insurance Company, and a

Continued

Financial Services Professional offers securities products & services through NYLIFE Securities LLC, (Member FINRA/SIPC), A Licensed Insurance Agency.*

In her role, she offers a variety of products that can help you meet a number of insurance and financial needs, including, but not limited to college funding, retirement, managing costs for extended periods of care and lifetime income strategies.

She enjoys traveling and is a happy wife and a proud mother to two amazing daughters.

*NYLIFE Securities LLC is a New York Life Company. One CityPlace Drive, Ste 260, Creve Coeur, MO 63141, 314-567-9080. Neither New York Life Insurance Company, nor its agents, provides tax, legal, or accounting advice. Please consult your own tax, legal, or accounting professionals before making any decisions.

Olga Sityaeva
314-363-0349
osityaeva@ft.newyorklife.com

Facebook: fb.me/OlgaSityaeva
Linkedin: linkedin.com/in/olya-sityaeva-48343836/

Yin and Yang

Following My Inner Voice

I have to admit I felt a bit intimidated writing a chapter in a book filled with so many inspiring stories. A year into my journey as a business owner, most days I am grateful if I can pay my office rent and not dip into savings to cover family expenses. But I've also realized over this past transformational year that I'm not only incredibly inspired myself, but have an inspiring story to tell, too.

In 2016, after thirty years of working as a nonprofit executive for multiple organizations in three different cities, I finally found the courage to firmly plant both feet—and my full determination—into starting my own consulting business.

I didn't know how much I knew when I started, and as I look back on my journey I've come to realize that the YIN of what I knew carried me into my present.

I've learned just as many lessons from good bosses as bad ones. Most good bosses see their imperfections and strive to do better. As a result, their organizations grow and thrive as everyone feels valued and each person contributes in their own unique way to the greater good. Most bad bosses project perfection and invincibility to such an extent that they stifle their employees' best work, create an atmosphere of fear, and if there is success, credit is taken by those in charge. I knew I wanted to give credit where credit was due.

My privilege is making a living while improving the world. The world is full of generous, caring, and inspiring philanthropists who truly can change the world. Working with thousands of philanthropists over thirty years in a multitude of nonprofit organizations, whose gifts ranged between eighteen-dollars and millions, has shown me that it is not the size of the gift, but the size of their hearts that move them to give to the best of their capacity. THAT is inspiring.

My reputation, credibility, and willingness to go the extra mile set the tone for every experience. As a professional staff member, I am the conduit and facilitator between the organizations I serve and the donors I am privileged to work with. It is never about us—it is always about the donors and the mission-focused work of the organizations that matter most.

My colleagues who have worked in the philanthropy world long enough know this and have their own stories to tell. It is a profound privilege to work with a major donor who is contemplating a transformational gift to the organization you represent. Many times, I have sat in their homes, listened to their personal stories, and been moved to tears as I listen to their reasons for giving. I feel their trust in me that the organization I work for will use their generous gift for meaningful and important work. The imperative is clear—my integrity to do the right thing for that donor is everything, and I will do everything in my power to honor their intentions.

The yin and yang of philanthropic work is no money, no mission—no mission, no money. You need to have a compelling case for support or reason for donors to give in order to raise necessary funds and you must have funds to do mission critical work.

When I decided to devote full-time to being a nonprofit consultant, I knew I needed to leverage every relationship I had, network like crazy, and find ways to convince others that what I was selling was what they needed to buy. The power of networking and connecting has certainly proven to be true; however, none of my clients to date have come from those I "pitched." Rather, all of my clients have come from secondary referrals and the least likely of places and people.

I'm not the only women at RISE who has experienced this phenomenon. In fact, at a recent cocktail party, a group of us laughed about how we wrote the plan, worked the plan, and then threw it out when we realized it wasn't serving us. **All of us have learned that following our inner voice and doing what is most natural to us plays to our strengths and results in better business outcomes.**

Listening to my inner voice has provided the yang as I've continued to experience anxiety, resilience, and belief in myself on my path to success. I'm acutely aware that most successful entrepreneurs are incredibility curious; the discovery that feeding my curiosity and inclination to question could be rewarded—and even deemed necessary to finding my unique niche and the value proposition I offered to potential clients—was my Eureka moment.

As uncomfortable as it is to experience anxiety, it is through experiencing it and pushing through to the other side that we are able to grow and thrive. If we are being honest, women who start their own businesses often have anxiety in abundance. They simply know how to harness it. I've learned to cope and problem-solve in the face of unexpected events. Nothing goes the way the written business plan says it will. If parts go as planned, consider yourself lucky.

Risk-taking, even with all its uncertainty, is the only path forward. I know that my resilience is my ability to problem-solve and advocate for myself. THIS is what we need in abundance from the moment we wake up until we finally go to bed at night. We must be willing to retrain our brain and belief system to understand that even if a situation becomes uncomfortable we can move through it.

Believing that I possessed knowledge and skills valuable enough that others would want to hire me took a huge leap of faith. My insecurities would creep up at the worst times, in the most unsuspecting ways, to keep me on a collision course to failure. That old self-fulfilling prophesy. Believe bad things will happen and they do. Conversely, when yin and yang come into play that self-fulfilling prophesy becomes a great thing—when you believe good things will happen and they do.

Reflecting on my new posse of brave, inspiring, and smart women who have made RISE their professional home, I know that I am not alone in experiencing this either. Depending on the day, one or more of us goes out into the world for a potential new client meeting, full of equal parts hope and uncertainty. Right before we go, as easy as a swipe of lipstick we say to one another, "You got this," and usually, we do, and we celebrate afterward.

Ego is necessary to believe in oneself and to attempt to do things others might discourage. Ego is what often drives that sense of urgency to keep things moving with the patience and quiet confidence to deal with setbacks. Ego and humility are the combination of seemingly opposite characteristics that prove the most valuable.

Tied to this is a willingness to own your mistakes as well as give credit where credit is due. It's not about you. There is no limit to the amount of good you can do if you don't care who gets the credit.

Humility, when witnessed in others, is often accompanied by being trustworthy and fair. These are the leaders who talk the talk and walk the walk. They value and practice servant leadership, viewing their role as that of serving the team. By asking employees what they need and then listening and responding as closely as is reasonable and fair enables everyone to win.

The yin and yang of being a woman in business offer contrary forces that I have found to be complementary, interconnected, and interdependent.

As women in business, our name and our work are our brand. The self-awareness to build on our unique strengths and the ability to leverage them as a business idea, combined with determination and grit to push forward with the integrity and humility to truly get to the heart of client needs, are key.

My job is to deliver the best outcomes for my clients. My reward is the deep satisfaction experienced when I meet my client needs and the internal validation that comes from knowing my strengths and leveraging them to achieve the greater good. If I can make a living doing this, I'm happy. My inner voice has never steered me wrong when I have been patient enough to quiet my mind and listen. Hence, the yin and yang.

Kristi Meyers Gallup has 30 years of fundraising experience across multiple nonprofit sectors, having served in a variety of executive roles for organizations including Washington University, Case Western Reserve University, University of Missouri-St. Louis, Jewish Federation, The Sheldon and Covenant Place.

In 2016 Kristi began devoting full-time to her consulting firm, Your Philanthropy STL, leveraging her extensive experience in annual, major, and planned giving, including work on multiple capital campaigns, to help her clients reach their fundraising goals. Her approach is to conduct an objective assessment which identifies opportunities for cost-effectively increasing contributed income. Kristi understands that it takes solid strategic planning, strong volunteer and executive leadership, and positive dynamics and messaging to effectively match donor interests with mission-critical activities.

Continued

Kristi has a Bachelor's of Journalism from the University of Missouri and a Master's in Nonprofit Management from Case Western Reserve University. She serves on the boards of the Association of Fundraising Professionals and the St. Louis Planned Giving Council.

Kristi has been married to her husband Ted for 32 years and has an adult son, Sam. When she is not working with clients, she enjoys hiking, yoga, reading, culinary pleasures and spending time with friends and family.

Kristi Meyers Gallup
kristi@yp-stl.com
yourphilanthropystl.com

Afterword

The Epigraph of this book began with one of my favorite passages by Marianne Williamson. It is a beautiful passage that especially resonates with me when she taps into that universal feeling of self-doubt. Williamson writes: "We ask ourselves: Who am I to be brilliant, gorgeous, talented and fabulous?" As I navigate the early days of my career path, I have had many moments of fear and self-doubt, as I suspect you have at some point, too.

But I love that the 17 women in the book you just read chose to take William's words to heart. Instead of giving into the temptations of fear, they ask in return, "Who am I *not* to be?"

Luckily, I was introduced to this brave way of thinking early in my career through a college internship with Stacy Taubman during the initial planning phases of RISE Collaborative Workspace. Almost every day that summer, we had coffee meetings with various impressive women in St. Louis. After each and every meeting, I left feeling inspired and honored that I got to hear their stories, some of which you read about in this book. And while I didn't know it at the time, this internship dramatically shaped who I was and who I would become.

Most importantly, I learned that defining and growing your community is essential to your success. You cannot succeed without the women around you succeeding.

At the end of that summer internship, RISE Collaborative had not yet opened, but I knew it wouldn't be long before this dream became a reality.

Three years after that fateful internship, I have come full circle. I am now the Community Manager at RISE Collaborative and having been there from the earliest stages, I can honestly say the reality is even better than the dream. Stacy and Kate have built a community of dynamic and impressive women. RISE Collaborative has become so much more than just a place to work. Our members thrive personally and professionally being surrounded by like-minded women who encourage their career growth, and make connections which support their success. It's a place to focus on their business, host meetings, and get it all done.

At the time of this publication, RISE Collaborative's doors have been open just one year and the growth of community I have seen already has been astounding. Our nearly 200 female members are the secret to RISE's success. They all the share the vision and dream that Stacy had for creating a strong cohesive community where women support other women. If you too want to become involved in RISE's growing community and learn more about our journey, visit us at RISEworkspace.com.

Rian Edwards
Community Manager